The Eldritch Plays

Eric Woolfe's

THE ELDRITCH PLAYS

STRANGE & EERIE MEMOIRS OF BILLY WUTHERGLOOM

GRENDELMAUS

SIDESHOW OF THE DAMNED

The Eldritch Plays
first published 2004 by
Scirocco Drama
An imprint of J. Gordon Shillingford Publishing Inc.

Scirocco Drama Series Editor: Glenda MacFarlane
Cover design by Doowah Design Inc.
Author photo by Helen Tansey
Printed and bound in Canada

We acknowledge the financial support of the Manitoba Arts Council, The Canada Council for the Arts and the Government of Canada through the Book Publishing Industry Development Program (BPIDP) for our publishing program.

Eric Woolfe
eric@eldritchtheatre.ca

Canadian Cataloguing in Publication Data

Woolfe, Eric
The Eldritch plays/Eric Woolfe.
Contents: Sideshow of the damned—The strange and eerie memoirs of Billy Wuthergloom—Grendelmaus.
ISBN 0-920486-55-X

I. Title. II. Title: Sideshow of the damned. III. Title: The strange and eerie memoirs of Billy Wuthergloom. IV. Title: Grendelmaus.

PS8645.O65E44 2004   C812′.6   C2004-902565-1

J. Gordon Shillingford Publishing
P.O. Box 86, RPO Corydon Avenue, Winnipeg, MB Canada R3M 3S3

Contents

A Reluctant Introduction

I first met the callow Master Woolfe when he approached me as something of an adoring fan, having been a devotee of a wee genre picture I had raised from the dust-bins of low-budget obscurity with my thespic slumming. I forget the name of the thing, but it was an absurd and pointlessly bloody video nasty about a woman who shattered her husband's brain with a television remote and then raised him back from the dead as some kind of contagious, cannibalistic zombie. As a result of my performance as a latter day Van Helsing in this crock of tripe, Master Woolfe alluded I would be the perfect scribe to pen the introduction to his morbid collection of ghastly juvenilia.[1] I foolishly agreed, under the grotesquely naive assumption that in order to be published, a playwright must meet certain moral, and artistic standards.

Let me say from the outset that the plays (if such frivolous schauerspieles can be called such) contained herein are little more than shallowly exploitive, gore hungry, sexually soporific, exercises in sepulchral stupidity. Woolfe can't focus his work or discipline his impulse to cavort with black comedy. For self-promoting "masterpieces of the macabre" to work on stage, there must be a serious tone for forays into the irrational, repressed, and shadowed aspects of humanity. But Woolfe's tone becomes unhinged, as, likely, is Woolfe himself. He thinks art ought to be funny, terrifying AND meaningful, rather than simply Artistic.[2]

[1] Mr Pomeranski isn't being really fair here. We met at Suspect Video in Toronto. He was trying to move their copy of this movie he's talking about to a more prominent space on the wrack, doubtless to attract more renters. I noticed the title and said, "Hey! 'Cannibal Undead Honeymoon' I've seen that" which I had, because my friend Burgandy Code plays a zombie stewardess in it. He got very excited and said, "You have! Oh, my! I'm in it you know. It's the only work I've done in years! And I played Lear in Drury Lane!" I mentioned that I was an actor too, and something of a playwright, and I had a collection of my work coming out. And he begged me—BEGGED ME—to let him write the introduction. "Help increase my profile with the younger set, you see. Let the world know I'm more than just a fading Shakespearean." And, it's not like I could say no to Neville Pomeranski, even if he is only a shadow of his former self.

[2] Well, that's true.

Let me deal with each grim travesty in turn...

Sideshow of the Damned[3] is a sickeningly demented romp that takes everyday situations and twists them into disgusting little schlock shockers. Although it is void of morality, solemnity or lofty aspirations, it does contain: a leering circus barker, a stabbing, a mutilation, a man disembowelled by his own prosthetic limb, a woman impregnated by half-human cockroaches, lycanthropy, hemeophagia, entomophilia, dismemberment, teen sex, adulterous sex, and undead sex, necromancy, not one but TWO severed tongues, another stabbing, lesbian nuns, a decapitation, a shark attack, an imp attack, a zombie attack and a non-lesbian nun attack and then winds up with another dismemberment and decapitation! And Woolfe has the audacity to call this Art?![4] Disgusting! In the early 1960s, on the West End, I was in the original English production of *Oh Zugzwang!*, in which two hoboes, who are encased to their necks in milk jugs, discuss existential angst and the true nature of God. Now that was Art!

I actually had some hope for *Grendelmaus*, in spite of rather odd allusions to *Beowulf* and *Moby Dick* that are spattered throughout the text. Unfortunately, the girl in the piece talks funny. However, I have heard that Master Woolfe was raised in a travelling carnival[5] and I assumed the circus argot to be genuine, if not dulcet to the ear. Still, it shapes out to be a nice romantic comedy until the end of the first act when a giant octopus demon pops out of a crock-pot, and before you know it, the girl in the piece is having relations with a giant, diabolic mouse! Why would anyone write such a disgusting thing![6] And I understand it was performed with puppets to boot! I hope no unsuspecting children wandered in off the street expecting some nice, family friendly Punch and Judy story only to be appalled with the sight of immorality and stupidity!

[3] I guess it's worth mentioning, since Mr Pomeranski doesn't, that *Sideshow* is my tribute to the EC comics of the 50s. And it was written in nine days on a dare.

[4] To be fair, I never called it "Art", I called it a "viscera-drenched phantasmagoria of giddy putridity".

[5] My father was an armless knife thrower, and my mother was a bearded lady. They retired when my dad was replaced by a knife-throwing human torso, and facial hair went out of fashion.

[6] Well, I wrote it because I thought it would be fun to work with Mary Frances Moore, who played the original Rachel.

The less said about *The Strange and Eerie Memoirs of Billy Wuthergloom*[7] the better. It's about a sexually stunted pubescent boy with a succubus under his bed. This work, I understand, was Woolfe's first attempt at playwriting. (Would that the Gods of Decorum and good taste stuck him down before he ever typed a word!) Here is where it all goes wrong. Most playwrights, when embarking on their freshman work, write about issues! About politics! Oppression! Things that matter to the society in which they live![8] Here we are faced with labyrinthine shopping malls and onanistic werewolves!

Doubtless Woolfe has his misguided champions. It has been said of him that he "writes like Edward Gorey drew" and that "No one can blend fantasy and reality quite the way Woolfe can." (As if psychotic hallucinations are now a virtue!!) He's been called one of the "few innovators in the theatre world" (Oh please!), "the master of the Suburban-gothic genre," (That's a genre?!) and (This seems most absurd of all:) "a delight!"

In conclusion, I must urge you. Toss this vile tome from your hands before reading another word; it is the strongest defence I know in support of book burning.

Sincerely,
Sir Neville Pomeranski
The Drake Hotel, 2004[9]

[7] I always admired Eric Peterson and John Grey for putting together *Billy Bishop Goes to War*. Here were these two friends, one an actor, one a musician, and they figured out this great way to hang out together and perform a wonderful play at the same time. So I wrote *Billy Wuthergloom* in order to chum around with my childhood friend, Marc Downing, who wrote the music and played the original Creepy Musician. As Marc was a childhood friend, I wrote a play about childhood and puberty. Because puberty really is scary, I wrote it as a horror play.

[8] I object to this! How can you say my work doesn't matter? If you had a succubus living under your bed, it would matter to you!

[9] This should tell you everything: Pomeranski does not live at the Drake Hotel! He's only saying that because it's supposed to be trendy now! He was thrown out of the Drake Hotel when they renovated, and now he's living on my couch.

Eric Woolfe

When Mr Woolfe was an infant he fell off the back of a gypsy caravan as it was passing through an ancient, primeval forest, at which point he was gleefully left for dead. Fortunately, he was raised in the wild by a family of foxes, who liked to make fun of him because of his last name. Having left the skulk at the age of fourteen to pursue his fame and fortune, he became an actor and playwright.

His other writing credits include *Dear Boss,* a Fortean investigation of Jack the Ripper, *Pomeranski Rex,* a hard-boiled Greek tragedy, and the upcoming *Chichimus Waylaid,* a musical written in collaboration with composer Allen Cole about witchcraft, murder and the early days of the CBC. His acting credits include *Dear Boss, The Lion King, Peter Pan, Grendelmaus, The Strange and Eerie Memoirs of Billy Wuthergloom, The Glass Menagerie, Kingdom of Earth, Picasso at the Lapin Agile, The Drawer Boy* and *Beyblade.*

He is also the artistic director of Eldritch Theatre, which was formed in 1998 after an impertinent Ouija Board informed Woolfe that his soul would be devoured by the Great Old Ones That Were And Shall Be Again unless he produced a series of puppet plays exploring the dark and foreboding mysteries of the Dread Necronomicon of Abdul-Alhazred. Unfortunately, none of these plays were ever performed, because when it came time to write grant applications, the Ouija Board would only spell gibberish.

Sideshow of the Damned

(A viscera-drenched phantasmagoria of giddy putridity!)

Characters

The Barker: a ghoulish narrator

Actor One (Male): Gogol/ Graham/ William/ Sister Ingrid

Actor Two (Female): Maddy/ Ezzy/ Imp/ Sister Mary-Frances

Actor Three (Male): David/ Harry/ Archy/ Jack

Actor Four (Female): Waitress/ Gloria/ Madge/ Shadowy Man/ Jenny

Of course, those are only suggestions. If a director wants to switch the doubling around, I have no objections, as long as the cast is made up of no more than four people plus the Barker.

Production Information

Sideshow of the Damned premiered on August 4, 2001, as part of the Summerworks Theatre Festival, Toronto, with the following cast:

BARKER .... Ron Kennell
ACTOR 1 .... Hume Baugh
ACTOR 2 .... Kimwun Perehinec
ACTOR 3 .... Darren Keay
ACTOR 4 .... Melody Johnson

Directed by Michael Waller
Gruesome Effects designed by Eric Woolfe
Stage Manager: Steve Minnie

The play was expanded and remounted at the Tim Sims Playhouse, Toronto, on October 17, 2002, with the following cast:

BARKER .... Steve Ross
ACTOR 1 .... Richard Allen Campbell
ACTOR 2 .... Kimwun Perehinec
ACTOR 3 .... Jason Charters
ACTOR 4 .... Rebecca Northan

Directed by Michael Waller
Gruesome Effects designed by Eric Woolfe
Stage Manager: Chris Dupuis

The theatre is dark and spooky. Strange music begins and a procession of ghoulish circus entertainers enter from the back. It is led by the BARKER—a hideous, lanky apparition with a bony face and top-hat, and malevolent, leering eyes. The creepy quartet carry a coffin, from which it will pull the props necessary to make the putrid performance possible…

I suppose it ought to be noted at this point that the horrors and bloodshed to follow should always be played stylistically, using half masks, red ribbons, and imaginative solutions in stead of the more costly latex, prosthetic and liquidy tricks utilised by the film trade. This is theatre, after all, and works best if the trickery is low tech, and its mechanisms are always in full view of the audience…

Where was I? Oh, yes. The grim processional winds it's way on stage and begins to set up, while the BARKER tells the tale to the audience.

BARKER: Step up! Ladies and gentleman!
The midway is closed for the night!
The Ferris wheel has turned her last!
The coaster's toast! Parades have passed!
The neon will no longer light!

Step up! My dams and my damned ones!
Your gentlemen escorts as well.
When the small and the big tops are dim,
Then darker exhibits begin.
Step up! to my Sideshow from Hell!

See! The axe of the poodle-head girl
Who hacked up her mother for bones!
See the heads of Two-Headed Roddy!
Two dollars more, we'll show you his body!
See the Living Dead Midget[1] Who Moans!

See! Our rank Egyptian Mummy
Who clawed her way out of her tomb!
See Moby Moe who grew so fat
Eating up children boiled in a vat!
See the Mirror that Shows You Your Doom!

Step up! Ladies and gentlemen!
Step up! Get in line while you can!
Step up! If you're brave and stout hearted!
There's no turning back once we've started!
Step up! for the Sideshow of the Damned!

The light shifts and…

[1] Ron Kennell, the Barker in the original production, insisted on saying, "The living dead little person who moans." It didn't scan as well, but maybe he was right.

Scene I: Climax Species

BARKER: Be silent! Hurl your bloodshot eyes this way and dip them in the crimson sop of our putrid display!

Hidden within these mildewed canvas walls crawl hideous aberrations too ghoulish to be believed. Their hideous mandibles snap and chaw! Their pink, fleshy, pincers twitch with vile corruption, as they slither over the hard ebon shells of their unearthly, hiving, abortive kindred! Creeping and skulking with their multiple limbs! they search ravenously for human viscera to lap greedily with their prickled! lulling! tongues! Don't quake, Madame! You're safe as long as you keep your hands away from the moist opening of their bejewelled grotto! O Sweet Jesu! I hear you cry! From what infernos, sullied pit did such monsters vomit forth! The answer can be found here! In this two-bedroom apartment, leased by a certain…

MADDY enters.

…Madeline Smith[2]—law student, aerobics instructor, and flawless specimen of human female perfection! A curvaceous, well-read zenith of Darwinian natural selection! With full, succulent breasts and strong, open hips!… But I run before my hearse, to the morgue.

The second bedroom! is let by a mysterious cripple who calls himself Doctor Gogol[3] Pomeranski! But his bed, a Spartan, pillowless plank dressed with one thin sheet goes unused! Because down this door here! We find a basement laboratory in which

[2] Named for the ingénue in Hammer's *Vampire Lovers*, and other such classics.
[3] Named for the Peter Lorre character in *Mad Love*, who for the love of a Grand Guignol actress sews murderer's hands on Colin Clive.

the doctor conducts his secret and macabre experiments, hidden away from the prying eyes of a world that is likely to ask too many questions too soon! and the ghoulish doctor knows only too well what trouble *that* can cause to the burning pursuit of mad science!

MADDY, who has been pouring herself a glass of orange juice, starts to scream in terror! The orange juice and empty jug fall and spill onto the floor. GOGOL comes running up from the basement. He is a twisted little man with a limp, an artificial, gloved hand and an opaque monocle on which is painted an open eye. He speaks in some vaguely European accent, which the linguists in the audience will recognise as lower Bosfordian.

GOGOL: Miss Madeline! Miss Madeline, what is it of the matter?

MADDY: Bug! Big bug! There! There!

GOGOL lovingly scoops the bug up and drops it gently into a Petri dish.

GOGOL: You poor lady. Did you running away from me? There, there.

MADDY: Is it one of yours? I almost stepped on it.

GOGOL: I am glad not. She is my mother-queen. Pregnant, see?

MADDY: Oh, no. Take it away! I—I'm sorry. But I just—I don't know how you can work with cockroaches all day long.

Shudders.

GOGOL: They are beautiful when you know them. Her shell, for example, has a hue of red to mix with the usual black. You see? She was brought to me from Kokovoko[4].

MADDY: It's very—um. Hm.

GOGOL: A good woman, she. Smart and strong, like you Miss Madeline. She has birthed a hundred of my new breed.

MADDY: New breed?

GOGOL: For my experiments. It is very technical.

MADDY: Ah. More power to you. They give me the creeps. I sure couldn't do what you do.

GOGOL: I doubt that, Miss Madeline. You could do anything. You could be a Queen.

MADDY: You're sweet.

GOGOL: Your juice? It has been spilled or drunk?

MADDY: Oh. I must have dropped it.

GOGOL: No, you sit. I make you more.

MADDY: You don't have to do that. I'm on my way out.

GOGOL: No. No. No. Sit. Sit. Sit. You need vitamins for healthiness.

He shepherds her into a seat, and mixes a jug of orange juice outside of her line of vision.

GOGOL: You're going out, you say?

MADDY: I'm meeting David. For dinner. I won't be late, I think.

GOGOL: I thought you and Mr Manners[5] were at an end. That's what you said.

[4] Kokovoko, incidentally, is the tropical island home of Queequeg, Ishmael's bosom companion in Melville's *Moby Dick*, used here because Neil Simon says the words with K sounds are inherently funny.

[5] David Manners played the bland and hapless hero in several Universal Horrors, including *Dracula and the Mummy*. He was blonde and bland and oh so ineffectual. He's retired now, living in California, and hates talking about horror films.

MADDY: Yes. Well. We are. I am. I haven't told him. I think it might be a shock, a little. Poor David. He really is a wonderful man. A lovely, wonderful, handsome man. I think he's pushing towards having a family and I can't— I'm just not— Mothering is not in me. The thought of some slimy pinkish thing growing inside you, yech.

GOGOL: It's a shame you and Mr Manners want so different, different things.

GOGOL drops some glowing liquid into the orange juice, which fizzes then subsides. He stirs it up, then pours MADDY a glass.

MADDY: Yes. It is a shame.

GOGOL: We must all do hard things for the greater good. Drink.

They fade away.

BARKER: Across town, a restaurant! Candlelit! French! Romantic to a fault! David Manners sits alone. Waiting. Waiting. Waiting...

DAVID: Waiter?

WAITRESS: Sorry to keep you waiting? Are you ready to order?

DAVID: I'm waiting for someone.

WAITRESS: A drink while you're waiting?

DAVID: No. Yes. Yes. Um. No... Wait.

WAITRESS: Oui?

DAVID: Can you—um—do me a favour? My—the woman I'm waiting for— It's sort of a thing, a surprise. Look. *(He takes a small box out of his pocket.)* A lady is going to join me. And when she does, please bring this out—um—on a tray with two glasses—a bottle of champagne. It's a surprise. See?

WAITRESS: Huh?

He opens the box. There is a ring in it.

DAVID: I'm going to propose.

WAITRESS: You're going to ask her to marry you? And I'll bring her the ring? *(She emits a long gleeful squeal!)* That's just so! *(She squeals again.)* Wow! You are SO romantique! I can't wait to tell them in the kitchen! *(And again.)* Oh my god![6]

DAVID: Okay then? Give her a minute to get settled, and then—

She takes the box. She squeals. She exits. DAVID takes a deep breath and waits. MADDY enters.

MADDY: Sorry I'm late.

DAVID: That's okay. It gave me time to get something straightened out.

MADDY: Hm.

DAVID: What?

MADDY: What what?

DAVID: You've got a look.

MADDY: Do I?

DAVID: Yeah… What?

MADDY: Nothing. No. Fine. There's nothing.

DAVID: …Okay.

MADDY: There's nothing.

DAVID: I said okay.

MADDY: Okay. I love you.

[6] I gave an anniversary present to an old girlfriend in this manner. She swallowed it.

DAVID: Okay. Good. Really good.

MADDY: David…? Why are all the waitresses looking at us?

DAVID: I dunno.

MADDY: Mm.

Silence.

MADDY: There's a problem.

DAVID: Oh shit.

MADDY: We need to talk.

DAVID: I'm gonna barf. I'm really gonna barf.

MADDY: We really, really need to talk.

DAVID: I— No. No… Nope.

MADDY: I'm sorry. About this David… I don't know—what to—how…

DAVID: Please hurry. Just say it. I'm going to be sick. and the sooner you say it, the sooner—

The WAITRESS enters with the champagne, the glasses and the ring. She's humming a snatch of Lohengrin.

Oh Christ.

MADDY: What going—?

WAITRESS: *(Squeals.)* Surprise!

MADDY: Are you— Is this?

DAVID: Please go.

WAITRESS: Quand?

DAVID: Just go.

WAITRESS: So-rry! *(She exits huffily.)*

A long awful silence.

MADDY: I don't know what to say.

DAVID: I—um… Go away.

MADDY: David.

DAVID: I—I—I…I want you to not be here. Now. Go.

MADDY: David, I love you.

DAVID: Maddy.

MADDY: I just—I can't be with you. It's wrong. We want so different, different things.

DAVID: No we don't.

MADDY: Yes we do.

DAVID: We don't.

MADDY: You want kids—

DAVID: Yes, so?

MADDY: —I don't think I do.

DAVID: You will. I'll wait.

MADDY: I don't see that for me. Maybe not ever. I have law school. And then I want—I have ambitions, dreams. I don't see a family in them.

DAVID: Maybe you'll change your mind. You're worth it to risk it.

MADDY: David. I don't want to be married. And I don't want kids. Ever. I will never want children.

Silence. Then DAVID starts flapping about to leave, throwing some bills from his wallet onto the table.

DAVID: Fine. Fine. Fine.

MADDY: David.

DAVID: No. Forget it… This isn't you.

MADDY: David.

DAVID: You changed. You're not you since this roommate—this " doctor"! *(The idea hits him.)* It's him, isn't it?

MADDY: No.

DAVID: Are you fucking him?

MADDY: Keep your voice down.

DAVID: Are you fucking him?

MADDY: No. It has nothing to do with Gogol. I don't want a family. Period.

DAVID: Maybe. But you're different since he moved in with you. You look different. You smell different.

MADDY: Don't be silly.

DAVID: I know your smell. It's different. It's more—I don't know—pheromony— He's done something to turn you against me.

MADDY: God, David.

DAVID: Do you know anything about him? Where he came from? References? What kind of doctor is he anyway, playing with bugs in the basement?

MADDY: Some kind of experimental entomologist or evolutionist or something?

DAVID: You have no idea!

MADDY: He is a brilliant scientist. He had to flee his country because a corrupt regime was clamping down on the intellectuals before the revolution. It's no big secret.

DAVID: I'm not leaving it at this.

MADDY: Yes. You are.

DAVID: I'm not.

He exits.

MADDY: David wait!

We are suddenly back at the apartment. GOGOL is comforting MADDY, who has been drinking.

MADDY: But he didn't wait, he just kept going.

GOGOL: You are too good for him. Scoundrel. You are better off without him.

MADDY: But I love him.

GOGOL: You do not. Change is difficult and ruthless. But the strong adapt. The strong evolve! The strong survive!

MADDY: Am I strong!

GOGOL: You are my queen!

MADDY: I am a queen.

GOGOL: Your drink, it is empty.

He pours her another, and quietly slips some of the strange liquid into her glass. She sips it. Then sniffs him.

MADDY: Hey, you smell pretty good.

GOGOL: Of what do I smell?

MADDY: I don't know. Good. You smell like sex. Before sex. Not after. You smell like before sex… I'm sorry. I can't believe I said that.

GOGOL: Drink.

She does.

GOGOL: Odour is a powerful force. The male cockroach seduces his mate by making a gift of his odour and his sperm.

MADDY: Really.

GOGOL: Yes. The male roach wraps his sperm in a membranous package called an oocthea. He scents the package with his own perfume then presents it to his prospective mate. If she covets the odour she accepts the gift. They wed, and couple, and breed forth a thousand young.

MADDY: That's so...steamy!

GOGOL: It is divine.

MADDY: Maybe I should slip into something more com— I'm going to put on my pyjamas now.

GOGOL: Yes. Good. Don't forgot your drink.

MADDY: See you later, alligator.

She exits into her bedroom. GOGOL quickly pulls some lethal looking scientific instruments from a hiding place. He fiddles with them. There is a knock on the door. He stashes them away.

GOGOL: A hundred curses!

More insistent knocking. GOGOL answers the door. It is DAVID. He brandishes some photocopied newspaper clippings

DAVID: You sick bastard! You thought you had us fooled, but I found you out Doctor Gogol Pomeranski! Or should I say Doctor Hjalmar Polzieg[7]! That's right,

[7] Boris Karloff's character in *The Black Cat*, who was in turned named for an architect particularly despised by the screen writer for having run off with his wife. Polzeig's a Satanic priest, a necrophile, a paedophile, a murderer and betrayed his unit to the Germans in WWI. Bella Lugosi skins him alive at the end of the film. It's a great little picture.

Polzieg, I know who you are, you butcher! I paid a little trip to the reference library and look what I found: You didn't flee your country because you were persecuted by the dictatorship! You worked for the dictatorship! You were their mad doctor, you tortured and maimed and vivisected all in the name of the dictatorship! Your name was feared and cursed and when the revolution came, the people set upon you! They came after you with knives and torches! It says here they killed you in very same dungeon you used for your atrocities! But it's wrong! You escaped, and you came here to continue you diabolic work! You bugbear! You bastard! You butcher! I'm going to tell Maddy! I'm going to tell the world!

GOGOL deftly slits DAVID's throat with a scalpel. Then he stabs out one of his eyes, chops off a hand, and pushes him down the basement stairs. He wipes the scalpel, and hides it just as MADDY enters. She's wearing a big, fluffy comfortable robe. Her glass is empty.

MADDY: Miss me?

GOGOL: I could think of nothing but your return.

MADDY: Empty.

She holds out her glass. He fills it with the strange liquid.

GOGOL: I made this especially for you.

She loosens her robe. She has lingerie on underneath.

MADDY: I couldn't decide how the evening was going to go. But I've made up my mind now. That last drink clinched it.

GOGOL: I see.

MADDY: What kind of science do you do, anyway, in the basement with the bugs, You Big Bad Bug Boy?

GOGOL: I study the future.

MADDY: The future of bugs.

GOGOL: The future of man.

MADDY: You have a nice eye.

GOGOL: Every ecosystem has its own evolution, its own climax species. In the beginning, the Great Old Ones ruled the wilderness, but they fell into deep slumber. The dinosaurs came but could not adapt. Then apes, and the apes evolved into man!

MADDY: You're cute when you talk all sciencey.

GOGOL: Man's time is coming to an end. When we die, ravaged by mutant diseases! When the ecosystem has been pushed too far and can no longer sustain us, what will survive? What species will rule the world for all time to come?! The Cockroach! The cockroach is the climax species!

MADDY: Ick.

GOGOL: If man is to survive, Man and the Roach must become one! And now at last, my Queen, your night has come! I will lay the foundations of the Superspecies in your strong womb! Tonight I will impregnate you with my scientifically engineered oocthea and a colony of Roach-Men will be conceived inside your strong womb! At last! At long last!

MADDY: You're mad!

GOGOL: That's what the revolutionaries said.

She stands to strike him, but GOGOL's drugs are too powerful. She passes out. He turns his back to her, and begins mixing liquids and setting up ferocious looking instruments. Scary organ music. Lightning flashes! We see the hideous impregnation experiment carried through a series of shocking tableaux. Underneath...

BARKER: Can there be any sight in the world more beautiful than a romantic autumn night, during which a young couple—spurred by romance, mutual attraction and wine—bring their bodies together in throbbing, sweaty ecstasy and from the sweet alchemy of their love conceive a beautiful new life?! Look at them! Doesn't it make you feel all warm and smooshy inside?

GOGOL: It is finished! Now I know how it feels to be God![8]

As he completes the final step, a battered, gore-covered DAVID sneaks up behind him. GOGOL finishes, and smiles just as DAVID disembowels him from behind. Much gore.

DAVID: You bastard! You meddled in God's domain!

GOGOL: You're too late.

Dies. DAVID revives MADDY.

DAVID: Maddy! Maddy! My God Maddy! What has he done to you? Are you okay?

MADDY: David? Oh David. David, I'm pregnant. He made me pregnant. Monsters are inside me. I'm going to be the mother of monsters.

DAVID: Don't worry, Maddy. We'll get rid of it.

MADDY: Not "it", David, Them. Hundreds of them. Maybe thousands. I can feel them squirming already. Thousands of larvae in my womb. My children.

DAVID: You can have an abortion.

[8] A line cut from 1931's *Frankenstein* for being sacrilegious.

MADDY: No David. I'm keeping them. You were right. I do want to be a mother. We're going to have a family.

Fade to black.

Scene II: Tarot of Terror

BARKER: And now, ladies and gentlemen, as a wise soothsayer once uttered, "We are all interested in the future because that is where you and I...are going to spend the rest of our lives!"[9] and so! Where would any ghoulish Side Show be without a hoary Gypsy Fortune Teller whose withered and gnarled hands can trace the convoluted creases upon your sweaty palms and draw from that hachure a foggy augury of your fortune. Or your doom. Thus! allow me to draw your attention to this curtain! Behind which, those souls among you bold enough to enter, will find a soothsayer and her swain in mortal need of a sibyl of their own!

A woman, EZZY[10]*, sits alone in a small tent. She is youngish, but hardened before her time. She is surrounded by the kitschy trappings of the faux-psychic. She is waiting anxiously for someone or something.*

EZZY: C'mon. C'mon. Christ in a suit. C'mon.

HARRY[11]*, a big, brutish, bruiser enters from outside. He's out of breath.*

HARRY: A couple is comin', Ezzy. Just like you was wantin'.

She peaks outside.

EZZY: Harry? You sure it isn't cops?

[9] Criswell in *Plan 9 From Outer Space.*

[10] Named for the Gypsy in *Notre Dame de Paris.*

[11] Named for our hamster, who's just as vicious, mean and blood-thirsty as his namesake.

HARRY: No, Ezzy. They's a young couple. Holdin' hands and moonin'.

EZZY: Okey, Harry. Git behind this curtain an' stick to the plan.

HARRY lingers guiltily.

EZZY: I said, git. *(Pause.)* You don't remember the plan, do ya?

HARRY: Maybe if you just give me a bit of a refresher.

EZZY: If you wasn't so good in the sack, I'd oust ya Harry, I would. You remember we robbed a store today, right? *(He nods.)* And you remember you killed the store guy an' his old lady?

HARRY: I sure do! He sassed you an' so I picked him up in my hands—

EZZY: Your big hands—

HARRY: An' I pulled his arm right off it's shoulder—

EZZY: And it made a beautiful ripping sound!

HARRY: Then I stuffed it down his throat and he couldn't breath no more.

EZZY: And he croaked.

HARRY: An' he turned blue and then he croaked.

EZZY: And his wife?

HARRY: Oh, I offed her for the fun of it. I never killed a dame by running her through a meat grinder before. It was tasty, huh?

EZZY: That's right Harry, it was yum-yum delicious. and now we got their money and we're rich but we need to split the country and go over the border, right? So we'll be safe.

HARRY: Home free.

EZZY: That's right, because Kokovoko don't got no extradition treaty. But to cross the border we need ID.

HARRY: I gots ID. I got a video membership.

EZZY: We just killed two people and emptied their safe. The cops is gonna be watchin' for people with *our* ID at the border. Right?

HARRY: Right! So we need ID from other people so we can pretend not to be us!

EZZY: Good boy! So, a young couple's comin', I'm gonna pull my gypsy psychic bullshit on 'em and tell their fortunes, and when they get up to leave here—

HARRY: I kill 'em both to death with my big big hands!

EZZY: Oh God, Harry. You got the biggest, big hands I ever seen on a fella. The biggest big hands I ever knew. Big big big big big hands. and I've known a lotta big big hands, Harry Honey. A whole big whapping big bag-full of 'em.

HARRY: *(Slowly, with terrifying menace.)* You mean you known a lotta big handed fellas? You never told me that before. If I'd a known that—

EZZY: *(Panicked.)* Don't be silly, Silly. I don't mean it like that. I'm a fortune teller is all. Guys come in here to get their palms read so I see their hands that way. That's all I was meanin'.

HARRY: *(Pause.)* Okay. I love you Ezzy.

EZZY: Me too, Harry. Now git behind the curtain.

HARRY: I just needed a reminder so I remember.

HARRY: One thing I don't get.

EZZY: What, Harry?

HARRY: You ain't really no gypsy, is ya? Cuz my folks don't approve of no cross-gentrification.

EZZY: No, Harry, that's just pretend. People trust a fortune teller better when they think she's gypsy.

HARRY: I get it.

EZZY: Good. Quick! They're comin'! Hide!

HARRY hides just as a young, attractive, completely average-looking couple enter. His name is GRAHAM INGELS. Her name is GLORIA PLATT[12].

EZZY: Come in, come in! Welcome! By Joshua, Judges, Daniel and Ruth, you seek to see, I say the sooth! I am Ezmerelda, I cast tarot! I read palms! I divine the mystery of the crystal ball! Come, come, come.

GRAHAM: Great. We'd—uh—we'd like to have our fortune told—

GLORIA: Wait, Graham. Are you a—a real gypsy?

GRAHAM: Not, well, not to be racist or anything—

GLORIA: Right. It's just that—

GRAHAM: Well, that—

GLORIA: That we've heard, you know.

GRAHAM: Gypsies—

GLORIA: Real ones.

GRAHAM: Are just better at the, the, the—

[12] Ghastly Graham Ingels was my favourite illustrator for EC Comics. He specialized in rotting corpse-flesh and other sepulchral sundries. Sadly, being a strict Catholic, he was deeply troubled by his artistic creations, and turned to the bottle for solace, which eventually ruined his career. Platt is Boris Karloff's actual surname. He was born William Henry Platt, and drove truck here in Canada for a while. Gloria Graham is a favourite actress of mine. I don't think she ever worked in the horror genre, but she was awfully cute all the same.

GLORIA: Gypsies are just better fortune tellers. That's all.

GRAHAM: That's what we've heard.

GLORIA: Yeah. No offence.

EZZY: I am a gypsy. Both my father's line and my dam's. She bore me at the crossroads. May the spirits of fortune tear my poor limbs asunder if I'm not a gypsy pure!

GLORIA: That's good enough for me.

GRAHAM: Right. What do we, ah—

EZZY: Tell me first a little of who you are, that I might see clearer into the future of your plight.

GLORIA: Um.

GRAHAM: Well—

GLORIA: Like, just tell you-

GRAHAM: Yeah, because, you know. It wouldn't be like very—like—fortuny—

GLORIA: Psychical.

GRAHAM: Yeah, psychical, if we just came out—

GLORIA: And poof! There's our whole problem on the table. Where's the divination in that?

EZZY: Oh, my poor young ones, with so little faith. You needn't fear. You needn't tell poor trust-worthy Ezmerelda more than you wish. I see all. I know all. I ask for merely an idea of your ID—I— I—identities. Your names. Where you come from. So I may ask the cards to clearly limn your problems to me.

GRAHAM: Well—

GLORIA: Fine. Okay.

GRAHAM: Fine. My name is Graham Ingels and this is Gloria—

GLORIA: His fiancée.

GRAHAM: My fiancée, Gloria Platt. Is that enough?

EZZY: For now. *(She shuffles a tarot deck.)* Cut, please, together. With the matter that troubles you foremost in your mind. *(GLORIA cuts the cards. Then GRAHAM. And EZZY deals a couple of them.)* Hm. Yes. I see.

GLORIA: What?

GRAHAM: What's there?

EZZY: You come to me because you fear there is…?

GRAHAM: Trouble?

EZZY: Yes, trouble in…the…way…of…

GRAHAM: Our marri—

GLORIA: Shh!

EZZY: I see trouble in the way of your marriage! *(She deals, with one eye on the couple.)* A force…events…a person…people… You fear that people seek to prevent your union!

GLORIA: Yes!

GRAHAM: That's—

GLORIA: How did you know?

EZZY: To one of gypsy blood, the cards tell all!

GRAHAM: Wow.

GLORIA: Well.

GRAHAM: Wow. Is there anything there about my, well, my family?

EZZY: *(Dealing.)* Yes! Yes! Master Ingels I see that your family is very important to you!

GRAHAM: Uh-huh!

EZZY: And that yours, Miss Platt is… *(Looking carefully at GLORIA, who is frowning slightly.)* Not!

GLORIA: You're right. Well, that is—

GRAHAM: She doesn't really have a family.

GLORIA: Any more.

GRAHAM: Right any more. They all died. Like, like—

GLORIA: *(Laughing a little.)* Oh god, like centuries ago! But his family—whew!

GRAHAM: Yeah, yeah! I come from like a really—I mean really—

GLORIA: His family is huge!

GRAHAM: Yup. Huge.

GLORIA: He's the—

GRAHAM: *(Slightly embarrassed.)* I'm the seventh son of the seventh son!

EZZY: The cards tell me that the size of your family contributes to your problem.

GRAHAM: No, well, yeah. Yeah. That's true. See, my family is, well—

GLORIA: Really religious!

GRAHAM: I'm not!

GLORIA: Oh no, he's not!

GRAHAM: Christ no.

GRAHAM: And being the seventh son of the seventh son—

Well, I was sort of a—

GLORIA: Obviously, he was totally an accident. Because his parents would never—

GRAHAM: Cuz, you know. And worse I was born on Christmas day. And that's—

GLORIA: Oo! Blasphemy!

GRAHAM: Right, like how dare I presume to be born on Christ's birthday!

GLORIA: Like he was the one who couldn't count nine months back from December.

GRAHAM: Right. So, I'm like the seventh of the seventh *and* born on Christmas day. So, as I'm sure you know...[13]

GLORIA: Being a gypsy and all—

GRAHAM: That comes with a...a...a...a...a...

GLORIA: Well, a certain—stigma.

EZZY: The cards tell me that your religious parents view you as the black sheep of the family. They fear that marriage with Miss Platt will exacerbate this matter because she also shuns your parents' faith!

GLORIA: You can say that again!

GRAHAM: Yeah, Gloria's totally against all that—

GLORIA: Don't say it!

GRAHAM: *(Whispers:)* Christ stuff—

GLORIA: All that iconography! Blech!

GRAHAM: Of like a bloody Jesus on a cross, or—

GLORIA: It's just unbearable, you know?

[13] See Hammer's *Curse of the Werewolf.*

GRAHAM: Or holy water, or anything churchy—

GLORIA: It just gives me the creeping willies. It does. Freaks me right out.

GRAHAM: Yeah.

GLORIA: Yeah.

GRAHAM: But of course, you know. You're a gypsy. Cuz of her name.

GLORIA: Right. I'm one of *the* Platts. The Platts of Old. Shudder! Oo!

EZZY: *(Dealing.)* Yes. I see it now. The Family Platt. Shrouded in mystery—and uh—bad—things. This, Master Ingels, this Platt thing, your family objects too as well.

GRAHAM: See, that's what rubs me raw. Because, of course! I mean, who else am I going to marry? Obviously, seventh of seventh, Christmas day! I'm going have difficulty finding a woman that—well—

GLORIA: Any other girl would just wind up dead.

GRAHAM: Right. Like, when I was eighteen I took this girl to the prom—

GLORIA: Sherry Lindstrom.

GRAHAM: Sherry Lindstrom. So, like, we dance. We drink. We go for a drive. There's fondling—

GLORIA: I'll just bet there was, you beast!

GRAHAM: Ruff!

GLORIA: Purrrrrrr!

GRAHAM: Hoooooooowl!!

GLORIA: God, you're sexy.

GRAHAM: Right. What. So. Petting. Sherry Lindstrom. Anyway, you know. A touch of flesh. A whiff a skin—and forget about that full moon crap. I just got hungry!

GLORIA: Who wouldn't?

GRAHAM: Right. You know, so, woof, ruffle, change, a little howling at the moon. I tore the top off her skull, ate her brain, and lapped the blood from her head like a cup.

GLORIA: It's going to happen.

GRAHAM: Right. Like it or not. It's going to happen. So, whatever my parents want, I'm never—I mean never—going to be suited for a white picket fence and a happy union with the head of the PTA.

GLORIA: Mm. Yummy PTA flesh! I'm starved.

GRAHAM: C'mon, hon. You said we'd have our fortune told first.

GLORIA: I know. I know. Let's just—

GRAHAM: Yeah. Right. So, finally after thirty-three lonely years I meet Gloria—

GLORIA: We were stalking the same prey! Isn't that cute!

GRAHAM: I pounced, she swooped down from nowhere!

GLORIA: Our eyes met! and powie! love at first sight.

GRAHAM: We shared the girl. It worked out well, because—you know—

GLORIA: I'm just after the blood, when all is said and done and Graham is—

GRAHAM: I'm more of a meat eater.

GRAHAM: But, I mean, we love each other, we're perfect together.

GLORIA: Werewolf, vampire. Vampire, werewolf.

GRAHAM: It makes perfect sense.

GLORIA: We both work nights.

GRAHAM: So, my question is: Will my parents ever see it our way, or is it a problem no matter how you slice them?

GLORIA: And hurry up, because after you're finished, we're going to eat you.

EZZY: Harry?! Harry, come out here please.

HARRY: Shh, Ezzy. I'm not supposed to kill them till you're done.

EZZY: We're done! Kill them! Kill them!

GRAHAM: Oh. That worked out well. One each.

GLORIA: Boy or girl?

GRAHAM: You pick.

GLORIA: No you.

GRAHAM: Girl?

GLORIA: Okay, Sweetie.

GRAHAM changes into a werewolf. GLORIA sprouts fangs. GRAHAM pounces on EZZY and shreds her. GLORIA swoops down on HARRY and takes a big gory chunk out of his neck. They feast. Then…

GRAHAM: Hey, does this taste like gypsy to you?

He hands GLORIA a hand. She takes a bite.

GLORIA: No.

GRAHAM: I didn't think so. Damn.

GLORIA: Don't worry, honey love. We'll find you some real gypsy tomorrow night.

GRAHAM: Promise?

GLORIA: I promise.

GRAHAM: I love you.

GLORIA: I love you too, snookums.

Blackout.

Scene III: Vow of Silence

BARKER: You! Stop smiling, sir! This isn't a frivolous entertainment! It has deep archetypal significance! Fine then. Laugh. But don't come crying to me, when you're seething in eternal perdition! The third dreadful display in our execrable exhibition, began ten years ago, with two wild and rebellious teenagers—one strapping boy! and one lovely girl!—left alone on a dark Friday night, without the staying hand of a moral chaperone to prevent them from doing what healthy teenagers do when unsupervised! and being young and curious and alone, they called forth the powers of Eternal Darkness!

Enter JENNY and JACK, two teenagers. He's frighteningly punk-gothic. She is a touch so, but not to the same extreme. He carries a knapsack.

JENNY: What is it, Jack? What is it you want to show me?

JACK: Are you sure you're mother isn't going to walk in?

JENNY: She'll be out all night with her boss. It's their third date. They rented the Kokovoko Suite at the Golden Pheasant Motel.

JACK: Okay then. Are you ready, Jenny? It's really scary.

He pulls some candles from his bag and sets them in a semi-circle.

JENNY: Ooh, candles. Whoopy doopy.

JACK: Not those, doofus. They're just for atmosphere. *(He lights them.)* Turn out the lights.

JENNY: I hope you're not going to whip out your thing and expect me to be all impressed.

She dims the lights.

JACK: If I did, you would be.

JENNY: No, I wouldn't, Jack.

JACK: Ya-a, Jenny.

JENNY: I felt it get hard when we were slow dancing at the semi-formal and it's no big whoop.

JACK: You did?

JENNY: Yeah. During the guitar part in *Stairway to Heaven.*

JACK: Ah, jeeze.

JENNY: It wasn't gross or anything. I thought it was pretty cool.

JACK: Mother o' Pete.

JENNY: It made me wet.

JACK: Yeah?

JENNY: Yeah. I thought it was sexy. I thought it was hot. *(She cosies up to him.)* I'm wet now. Wanna see?

JACK: Let me show you this first.

JENNY: You make me horny. I want to make you hard.

JACK: Stop it! I'm trying to show you something important! Jeeze.

JENNY: Well, sor-ry. I thought you'd want to, Erection Boy.

JACK: Cut it out. I do want to. Really. You make me horny too. I like you. You're sexy.

JENNY: There's nothing wrong with it.

JACK: We'll do it in a minute.

JENNY: Why don't we do it now, and then look at your surprise later.

JACK: Well, cuz, this way's better.

She gets very, very close.

JENNY: Better than this.

JACK: I dunno.

JENNY: How 'bout this.

She kisses him.

JACK: Maybe not.

JENNY: I think you like this better.

She starts to undo his belt, while kissing his neck.

JACK: Me too.

They kiss awkwardly but enthusiastically for a long time. Then JACK reaches up with both hands and grabs JENNY's breasts. JENNY jumps back, a little freaked.

JENNY: Let's see your surprise now.

JACK: In a minute.

JENNY: No. Now. I'm really curious.

JACK: Shh. You talk too much.

JENNY: If you satisfy my curiosity now, I just know I'll be more into it later.

JACK: But—

JENNY: Like, I'll be really, REALLY into it.

JACK: Really?

JENNY: Like, really!

He takes a large book out of the bag. It's written in blood and bound in human skin.

JENNY: Oh. My. God.

JACK: Do you know what it is?

JENNY: Is that...?

JACK: Yes.

JENNY: No.

JACK: Yes. It's the dread Necronomicon of the Mad Arab Abdul Alhazred![14]

JENNY: No!

JACK: Yes.

JENNY: The dread Necronomicon of the Mad Arab Abdul Ahazred?

JACK: Ya. I stole it from the locked glass case in the school library.

JENNY: It's dangerous. It's for reference only!

JACK: Does it excite you?

JENNY: No. It scares me. Put it away!

JACK: Know what we're gonna do with it?

JENNY: Let's not do anything with it. Let's have sex. I'm ready to go all the way.

[14] The dread tome that appears periodically in H.P. Lovecraft stories. Most of the incantations that follow are Lovecraft's as well.

JACK: Don't be such a chicken. There's an incantation in it that will imbue us with the power if the Great Old Ones That Were and Always Shall be!

JENNY: Jack, this isn't right. There's a reason they took that book off the study list!

JACK: We'll be immortal! We'll be omnipotent! We could murder all our teachers in their beds and no one would know anything! Even if they kill us they couldn't stop us. You could pull out Mr Enright's liver with your bare hands!

JENNY: Mr Enright's not so bad.

JACK: He won't let us play cards in the cafeteria![15]

JENNY: That's no reason to ask the Goat With A Thousand Young to disembowel him!

JACK: C'mon, it'll be fun!

JENNY: Jack, don't. I mean it.

JACK begin to read.

JACK: I R'lyeh Cthulhu f'tagen. Ia! Ia!

JENNY grabs him. He pushes her off.

Yai 'Ng Nga!

She grabs him again. He hits her with full force. She falls back.

Yog-sothoth!

Scary creatures become dimly visible in the darkness.

JENNY: Jack stop!

She grabs at the book. He wrestles her down.

[15] Real teacher. I had him in high school. He was strictly religious and believed playing cards would lead to gambling, so—and I'm not making this up—we shot craps instead.

JACK: N'gah-Kthun! Nyarlathotep!

JENNY: I'll tell! I'll tell everyone what you've done!

JACK: Ia Shub Niggurath!

JENNY: I'll tell your father!

JACK: You wouldn't!

JENNY: I will if you don't stop!

JACK: Oh no, you won't!

He pulls some scissors from his bag. They skirmish. He forces her to the ground and cuts off her tongue, which he then throws aside. Blood streams from her mouth.

Now you won't tell anyone anything. *(He returns to the book.)* Rezol Evob Gybb![16]

JENNY stabs JACK with the scissors repeatedly.

I'll get you for this! I will!

He dies. She cuts out his tongue. The creatures from the darkness come and carry him away.

BARKER: I know. I know. It's shocking, but if you heard the music that these kids listen to you wouldn't be surprised. Entertainment is much too violent these days... Time flows on like blood from an open throat. Three years later! The Sisters of Saint John the Dwarf[17] Holy Convent have a new novice join their cloister. Sister Jenny is a wan girl, with haunted eyes and a troubled past. She's also had her tongue torn from her throat, but given the

[16]Not Lovecraft. This is from *The Muppet Show,* ostensibly an ancient Egyptian curse. Anyone who uttered it was immediately swallowed by an alligator puppet.

[17] A real saint, circa 4th century. He was ordered by the chief abbot to water a walking stick that the abbot had stuck in the dirt. John did, every day, walking four miles back and forth to the well. On the third year, the walking stick bore fruit, with which the abbot fed the cloister, proclaiming, "Behold! The Fruit of obedience!"

order's vow of silence, no one seems to notice much.

Inside the Holy Order of the Sisters of Saint John the Dwarf. Beautiful organ music plays.

SISTER INGRID, SISTER MARY FRANCES, and SISTER JENNY enter.

They kneel, genuflect and pray.

SISTER INGRID emits a rolling, thunderous fart.

SISTER MARY FRANCES and SISTER JENNY exchange glances and begin to giggle. Quickly, they cover their mouths to stifle the sound.

SISTER INGRID glares at them, then exits huffily.

SISTER JENNY and SISTER MARY FRANCES look sheepish.

INGRID returns with a lethal-looking stick.

SISTER JENNY rises, and offers her hands.

SISTER MARY FRANCES does the same, with attitude.

SISTER INGRID whacks JENNY's palms, then whacks the palms of SISTER MARY FRANCES.

SISTER JENNY offers her hands again. She wants more.

SISTER INGRID exits, disgusted.

SISTER MARY FRANCES shrugs. Waves at JENNY, flirtatiously. Exits.

SISTER JENNY prays fervently. Soon she pulls a strop from her habit and flagellates herself.

An eldritch chanting rises from the shadows. Words from the dread Necronomicon of the Mad Arab

Abdul Alhazred are sounded by vile, susurrus voices.

SISTER JENNY rises, afraid. Something is coming for her, but where?!

A hand reaches for her from the shadows, grabbing her shoulder from behind.

SISTER JENNY whirls to see…!

SISTER MARY FRANCES enters.

JENNY is about to club her!

The nuns almost scream, but cover each other's mouths just in the nick of time!

They realize they are safe and relax.

SISTER JENNY starts to cry and falls into SISTER MARY FRANCES's arms.

SISTER MARY FRANCES starts to rub her back. Her touch grows longingly romantic. She kisses SISTER JENNY's cheek, quickly. Then her forehead. Then her lips. Then her lips again, passionately.

SISTER JENNY appears to return the kiss at first but suddenly she pulls away.

SISTER MARY FRANCES looks hurt.

SISTER JENNY invites her to pray.

SISTER MARY FRANCES rolls her eyes, and prays with her.

SISTER JENNY, thinks for a moment. Perhaps she feels a little guilty. Perhaps she's aroused. She starts to rub up against SISTER MARY FRANCES as they pray. The shoulder rubbing becomes slowly more intense, and erotic.

Unseen by the amourous nuns, dead JACK crawls ups behind them with scissors. He's grotesque and rotting, and doesn't seem at all friendly. He leaps up, in a silent, vengeful BOO!

JACK grabs SISTER MARY FRANCES violently, and drags her upstage.

SISTER MARY FRANCES screams and screams and scream as she is pulled away. She kicks and screams and screams and kicks…

JACK takes the scissors, astride SISTER MARY FRANCES and brings the open blade down upon her neck.

SISTER MARY FRANCES stops screaming and goes slack. Her head is cut clean off!

JACK turns to SISTER JENNY, holding SISTER MARY FRANCES's severed, bloody head in his hands. He throws it at her.

SISTER JENNY catches it. Drops it. It bounces back into her hands.

JACK stalks towards SISTER JENNY, scissors snipping, ready to kill her.

SISTER JENNY hikes up her habit and displays a beautiful, virginal leg.

JACK stops and briefly considers his options. Having giving it some thought, he raises up the scissors and jumps back in for the kill.

SISTER JENNY flashes her lovely bosom.

Her charming decolletage stops JACK in his tracks. He, puts down the scissors and falls adoringly into her breasts.

JENNY smiles cunningly, and stabs him repeatedly with the scissors.

JACK looks up, stunned, and then falls dead.

JENNY sadly moves to poor SISTER MARY FRANCES's severed, bloody head. She cradles it, lovingly.

SISTER INGRID suddenly enters, and surveys the scene, which you must admit, doesn't look at all well for JENNY. She points at the blood covered, head-carrying, scissors-wielding, mute JENNY.

INGRID: Mm! mmm! Mmm! mmm!

JENNY shakes her head. She steps towards INGRID holding the scissors and the gory head.

SISTER INGRID: Fuck Holy fucking fuck! You fucking killed them! You'll fucking burn in hell fucking fire, you fucking fucked up fuck!

JENNY shakes her head.

JENNY: Gna-mafa-gaaa!

SISTER INGRID: What the fuck?

JENNY tries some charades. Three words. Sounds like. Points to JACK's corpse.

SISTER INGRID bellows and lunges at her, stabbing JENNY with the scissors.

INGRID: Fuck! Fuckity! Fuck! Fuck fuck!

She realizes she has broken her vow of silence. She clamps her hands over her mouth. She gives JENNY the double finger and runs off.

JENNY has fallen near JACK's body.

Silence.

JACK's undead hand laboriously pulls itself to JENNY's lovely breast.

JENNY swats it away.

They die.

Again, JACK's hand laboriously pulls itself to JENNY's breast.

She swats it away.

They die.

Yet again, JACK's hand laboriously pulls itself to JENNY's breast.

She swats it away.

They die.

BARKER: The damnation of Jack and Jenny. It is the damnation of those who covet and lust after a booty that is ever out of reach. For who can imagine a torment more vile than that of Tongueless Jenny and Gory Jack, to be ever guided by raging pubescent hormones which, by supernatural perpetuation, live ever on after death. Striving, reaching, slapping down. To be forever and utterly be tagged out while steeling the pillow pleasures of second base! Can you imagine a torment more vile, Sir? Can you, I said? Can you? Can you?! Of course you can't, you idiot. But I can. And I'm going to show it to you now!

Scene IV: The Bottled Imp[18]

BARKER: Ladies and Gentleman, you will see two! strange things! The first! A small antique bottle, stopped with a blackened cork. The bottle is milk white and

[18] To the best of my knowledge, this idea first appeared in a Robert Louis Stevenson story. I've never actually read it.

nearly opaque, but the observant amongst you may notice that something moves mysteriously inside it, ebbing and flowing like shadow and fire. They say it once belonged to Genghis Khan and Napoleon and that its glass is indestructible and was forged in the very fires of Hell! At least, that's what they say. The bottle is the least interesting of our two exhibits. The second strange thing! sits beside the bottle, and…well…once you've seen it, there's little left to say, except perhaps, "My God, how can it survive in all that endless pain?"

The BARKER's flashlight illuminates the unclothed posterior end of WILLIAM, who is engaged in coital activity with MADGE, whose kicking heels are also caught in the flashlight's effulgence.

BARKER: It seems we have a Third Strange Thing.

MADGE: Come on and swing it at me, you sweat-soaked baboon!

WILLIAM: Oh, yeah. Oh yeah. I'll swing it. I'll swing it right at you, you bawdy hag!

MADGE: Oh.

WILLIAM: You slut-cake!

MADGE: Oh!

WILLIAM: You five and dime, cheese waxing, pigeon slapping tramp!

MADGE: Oh William! Yes! Yes you wreaking Neanderthal! Yes!

ARCHY enters. The weight of the world is already on his shoulders.

ARCHY: Madge!

MADGE: Archy!

WILLIAM: Archy?

ARCHY: William?

MADGE: William.

WILLIAM: Madge!

ARCHY: William!

WILLIAM: Archy.

ARCHY: Madge. William. *(To himself.)* Madge and William.

MADGE: *(As the adulterous couple buck themselves across the finish line.)* That's right Archy, Madge and William. William and Madge.

WILLIAM dismounts.

ARCHY: Tell me this isn't what it looks like.

MADGE: What does it look like?

ARCHY: It looks like my wife screwing my best friend.

MADGE: Yup. That's pretty much it.

WILLIAM: Well, we're not really *best* friends. Let's be fair, Arch. I lend you my tools, and we golf together but really!

ARCHY: How can you do this to me?

MADGE: We were doing it to each other, Archy. You just happened to walk in.

WILLIAM: *(To MADGE.)* Shouldn't he be at work?

MADGE: Yeah, why aren't you at work, Archy?

ARCHY: I was fired today.

MADGE: You were what?!

WILLIAM: Ooh, look out cowboy!

MADGE: Why did you do a stupid thing like that?

ARCHY: I didn't do it. Mr Gaines[19] did it. He said they have no further use for me.

MADGE: You fatuous moron! I told you he was going to get himself fired.

ARCHY: At least, I still have you.

MADGE: Archy, get real! I'm shtupping your best friend—

WILLIAM: Hey.

MADGE: —your close acquaintance. You don't have me. Ha! I can't believe you thought that! Dummy!

ARCHY: We have our home.

WILLIAM: *(Laughing.)* Oh, jeeze!

ARCHY: What?

WILLIAM: Did you forget to tell him?

MADGE: I was going to send him a postcard from the beach.

ARCHY: About what?

MADGE: You lost the house, Arch. The bank foreclosed.

ARCHY: What! We've been paying the mortgage!

MADGE: We haven't actually.

ARCHY: I gave you a cheque each month to deposit.

MADGE: I've been signing them over to William here. He is a wizard with a high-risk profile!

WILLIAM: I'm good in the sack too.

By way of agreement, MADGE puts her hands out, as if to describe a large trout.

[19] Named for William Gaines, editor of EC Comics until censorship pressure drove them to bankruptcy.

ARCHY: I don't understand.

MADGE: I've been steeling your money for William. He bought low, sold high. And now we have a nice bungalow in the Kokovoko Islands.

WILLIAM: The chicks go topless there.

ARCHY: We're going to the Kokovokos?

WILLIAM: He is *so* slow!

MADGE: No, Brainless. Just William and I. We hate you. You have no house. No wife. No job. You were born a loser and I don't like the way you smell.

WILLIAM: You can keep the tools I lent you though. See you, Arch.

MADGE: Love to talk, but our plane's in an hour. B'bye. We're taking the car.

ARCHY hands over the keys. WILLIAM and MADGE exit gleefully.

BARKER: As the knife-thrower's decapitated assistant observed, "Life can change in the blink of an eye." See how quickly it happens, Ladies and Gentlemen? One moment you're safe and cosy, cuddled up with your lover in your nice warm bed, and the next moment—you're Archy!

ARCHY: Buy a paper, help the homeless. Paper, lady? Hey buddy, want a news paper? They're printed on real newsprint.

A SHADOWY MAN enters.

ARCHY: Excuse me, sir. Would you like to buy a paper?

SHADOWY MAN: I'm not buying today.

ARCHY: This is a good issue. The ink hardly comes off on your hands at all.

SHADOWY MAN: I'm selling. Would you like to buy everything you ever dreamed?

ARCHY: If I could afford that, you think I'd be selling papers to the likes of you? *(He steps away.)* Buy a paper, help the homeless.

SHADOWY MAN: It's cheaper then you think.

ARCHY: I got five cents. It's cheaper than five cents?

SHADOWY MAN: That's too much. I can't take that much.

ARCHY: Look, I don't know what your game is, but I'm not a junky. I'm not a drunk. Whatever you're selling, take it somewhere else.

SHADOWY MAN: Please! I'm begging you. Just look at it. *(He takes a strange bottle from his coat.)* See? It can grant your every wish.

ARCHY: What's in it? Barbara Eden?

SHADOWY MAN: It's a bottled imp.

ARCHY: A what?

SHADOWY MAN: I'll sell it to you for two cents.

ARCHY: If it can grant my every wish, how come you're selling it so cheap.

SHADOWY MAN: The bottled imp will grant its owner his every desire. But if the owner still has possession of the bottle upon his death, he'll go straight to Hell, where demons will feast lasciviously on his tortured, Promethean flesh for all eternity.

ARCHY: So throw it away, off a bridge. Leave it on the subway.

SHADOWY MAN: I've tried. I even buried under the corner stone of the new museum. It always comes back. To get rid of it, you have to sell it.

ARCHY: Tried eBay? I heard some guy was selling his soul on that.

SHADOWY MAN: I have to sell it for less than I paid for it. That's the only way to get rid of it.

ARCHY: How much did you pay?

SHADOWY MAN: Three cents. I'll sell it to you for two. You can still get rid of it for a penny.

ARCHY: Please. I don't want any trouble.

SHADOWY MAN: Buy it from me! Buy it from me or I'll kill you! I'll kill you in ways you can't imagine.

ARCHY: Okay! Okay! Don't hurt me. Here. It's a nickel.

SHADOWY MAN: That's too much! I told you—

ARCHY: I don't have anything smaller. Sorry. Can you make change?

The SHADOWY MAN pokes through the change in his wallet. It takes forever.

SHADOWY MAN: There's… Um… Okay. There's one… One…Two… Two…and… There. There's three cents. Here you are, my friend. You are now the fortunate owner of a bottled imp.

ARCHY takes the strange bottle. The SHADOWY MAN starts to exit.

ARCHY: Hey Buddy? How do I open it? The cork is stuck.

SHADOWY MAN: The cork can never be removed. The bottle is sealed forever.

ARCHY: So, how do I work it?

SHADOWY MAN: Just call forth the imp.

Exits.

ARCHY: What the hey. Oly Oly Oxenfree, Mister Imp, come-out come-out where ever you are.

The IMP materialises. It's terrifying.

BARKER: If you listen very, very carefully… Wait… Shh… There, the only sound in the world is the panicked palpitating of Archy's trembling heart. Even the saliva in his mouth has stopped dripping.

A very lengthy silence. The hideous IMP stares at ARCHY, tilting its head ever so slightly back and forth. Finally…

ARCHY: I wish… I wish Madge and William would pay for what they did to me.

The IMP smiles. Blackout.

Lights up on a beach in Kokovoko. MADGE and WILLIAM frolic in the surf. A dorsal fin appears. Several more follow. MADGE and WILLIAM are devoured by sharks. The blue ocean runs red with blood. Blackout.

Lights up on ARCHY. The imp enters, carrying a bag of bloody body parts. He hands it to ARCHY.

Oh god! Is that— *(He turns away in disgust. He looks*

violently ill. Pause. He looks back into the bag.) Is that them? Yes, I think I recognise Madge's nose. Wait. That's not a— What is that— Yech! She was right, it is big. God. They're—they're really, really, really dead. That's —that's great! Good imp. Good boy. Um.

The IMP is just staring at ARCHY, waiting.

Well... I guess I'd like to be really rich.

The IMP turns to go.

Wait! For me to be rich, will something bad have to happen to other people. Like, will you kill lots of people and bring me their money? Or cause some awful blood soaked tragedy, that through some ironic twist of serendipity will end up in my becoming a millionaire?

The IMP nods.

Fine. Whatever. Money. Blood-money. Why be picky?

The IMP smiles and exits.

BARKER: And so our hero grew more and more rich and powerful with each passing wish! Soon! he had his every yearning! Soon! all the world trembled at his feet! Soon! He had become the most feared and terrible human being on the face of the scorched and blackened earth!

ARCHY: *(Who is dressed as a powerful ruler.)* Well, well, well! Here I am General King Papa Archibald Caesar the first! Sovereign dictator of the first and second world! You've done well for me imp! I've got riches, I've got munificence! Who could ask for anything more! If only Madge and William could see me now, that'd show them not to mess around with Archy!

The IMP smiles and exits.

Hey, where are you going. *(Pause.)* Hm. I hope he didn't think that was an actual wish. *(Pause.)* Nah. That wouldn't be fair. *(Pause.)* O holy crap fish. How could I fall for that old one? I'm such a dink!

There are scary sounds. Quiet at first, and then growing. Something is coming for ARCHY. A thump.

Who's there?

Another threatening noise.

Hello?!

DEAD WILLIAM: *(Off)* Archy!

ARCHY: William?

DEAD MADGE: *(Off)* ARCHY!

ARCHY: Madge?

Long, long wait for something scary to happen, while tension builds. Where are they coming from? Was it just the wind? Suddenly, from a surprise place the IMP enters.

ARCHY: Aah! Oh. Thank Saint Pete at the gate. It's only you.

The IMP smiles. Scary pause. Then, DEAD MADGE and DEAD WILLIAM enter. They don't look well at all. In fact, they look positively sickening. The imp watches, smiling silently.

DEAD WILLIAM: You wanted us to come and we're coming, Archy!

DEAD MADGE: We're coming slowly because little pieces of us keep falling off[20].

[20] A line proudly borrowed from EC's *Vault of Horror*.

DEAD WILLIAM: But we're coming! We're coming to get you!

DEAD MADGE: We're going to tear you to pieces, Archy! Like the shark did to us!

ARCHY: Ah! No! Please no! If I die now I'll go straight to hell!

DEAD WILLIAM: You should have sold the bottle Archy!

ARCHY: Wanna buy it? A penny! I'll sell it to you for a penny!

DEAD MADGE: The sharks ate my purse, Archy!

The fall upon him and begin to tear him to shreds!

ARCHY: No! No! I don't want to go to Hell! Please, Imp! I wish to live! I wish to live forever! I wish that no matter what they do to me, I'll never die!

DEAD MADGE: Little pieces, Archy!

She pulls off his head. They exit. ARCHY's body is in tiny pieces, scattered over the stage.

ARCHY's HEAD: Ow! Ow! Hey! That hurts! Wait a minute! I'm just a head! Hey, I'm in agony! How can I hurt this much and not die! Ow! Ow! OW!!!!!! Oh my god! This pain, this intolerable pain will last forever and ever and ever and ever and ever! Ouchy! Ouch! Yikes.

BARKER: One last peak, Poor Patron, to insure you've had your fill…

The cast poses ghoulishly!

Hopla! The Sideshow of the Damned is over! Leave now and never look back! Go! Leave! Go now! Go! Go! Go away! Leave! Now! Go. Boo!

The curtain slowly falls.

The End.

The Strange and Eerie Memoirs of Billy Wuthergloom

Production Information

The Strange and Eerie Memoirs of Billy Wuthergloom premiered on August 5, 1999, as part of the Summerworks Theatre Festival, Toronto, with the following cast:

BILLY .... Eric Woolfe
CREEPY MUSICIAN .... Marc Downing

Directed by Jason Charters
Music by Marc Downing
Stage Manager: Samara Nicholds

The play was expanded and remounted at Buddies in Bad Times Theatre, Toronto, on April 11, 2000, with the following cast:

BILLY .... Eric Woolfe
CREEPY MUSICIAN .... Marc Downing

Directed by Michael Waller
Music by Marc Downing
Lighting design by Rick Banville
Necromantic Witchery by Samara Nicholds
Stage Manager: Danielle Guillaume

Scene I

Lights up on a twisted expressionist world of childhood and terror, like a public school version of the Cabinet of Dr Caligari. *A gaunt, cadaverous musician horrifically lurks onto the playing area. He pulls back a curtain or opens a large trunk to reveal BILLY, who apart from a an unsettling, eerie pallor, is a young, nondescript man like any you would meet on the street.*

BILLY: *Singing:*

There's a monster in your closet
There's a goblin down the hall.
The sobbing noise you hear each night
Is the children in the walls.[1]

There's a witch who comes to get you
If you're not in bed by ten.
She has a smelly burlap sack,
And she'll try to stuff you in.[2]

There's a thing inside your toilet
And it doesn't have a name.
It reaches up and grabs your bum
And pulls you down the drain.

There's a scratching at your window.
Better keep the curtain closed
It's the man with ice for eyeballs
And a meat hook for a nose.

[1] A recurring nightmare of my mother's. I think it's pretty creepy too.

[2] A recurring nightmare of mine. Creepier. Most of these things are actually my real childhood bogies. Especially the toilet monster. He scared me bad.

And the pale woman is under the streetlight
And I know that she can smell you
No matter what your mommy tells you
The pale woman gets closer each night.

Spoken:

I've come to warn you there are shadowy things that we cannot see; grim unearthly creatures that prey upon us when we are weak and unsure and our bodies are changing. When you are a child, people always tell you that puberty is natural, don't be afraid. They lie. Puberty is supernatural. So be afraid. Be terrified. And pray the Things don't find you until long after your pubic hair has grown!

There's a banshee in your basement
Who's as black as she can be.
At night a dozen spooks sneak in
And sit on your couch and watch TV

There's a skeleton in your toy box
And his hunger grows and grows
Keep your feet under the blankets
His white teeth might bite off your toes.

There's a zombie in the floorboards,
And he's coming up for air.
A voodoo priest can enslave your soul
With just your toenail and some hair.[3]

Your Mommy and your Daddy
Cannot warn you, not a bit.
For they know the Demon Tailor
Will take some thread and sew their lips.

[3] Truth be told, I don't know if this is all a voodoo priest needs to enslave your soul, but Howard Hughes used to have Mormon servants collect his toenail pairings and preserve them in sealed mason jars, which he kept locked in a safe. And I figure he must have been afraid of something.

And the pale woman is under the streetlight
And I know that she can smell you
No matter what your mommy tells you
The pale woman gets closer each night.

My Mom and Dad always assured me there were no monsters, and I did my best to believe them, but I knew they were wrong. I could sense a diabolic presence under my bed. I could hear it breathing through the night in rhythmic, hissing rasps. I could hear it scratching its claws against the multi-coloured shag carpet. Only the dutiful guard of my brave teddy bear, Boogie[4], prevented the monster from devouring me in my sleep.

SUCCUBUS's VOICE: I'm going to suck your bones!

BILLY: I lived with this terror till my eighth birthday. For my best friend Sander Poochila's birthday, six of us went to his house for a sleepover. Then my other best friend, Boker Tunkman, had a sleepover when he turned eight. So when my birthday rolled around, my mother suggested I have a sleepover too. My gorge rose! Boogie could successfully defend me from horrific dismemberment, but was he powerful enough to protect seven cake-fed revelers from this vicious Grendel? On the other hand, if I chose not to throw a sleepover, all my friends would call me a weenie.

My Grampa always said: "To answer the strange, look to the more strange."[5] And the strangest person in all of Wanlend Heights Public School was a wormy little boy named Hirskill Fischmascher. Hirskill Fischmascher was a Two Name Person. Most people are only One Name

[4] My real teddy bear. He played himself in the original production. I wrote the part for him.

[5] Actually the slogan of the medieval alchemists, who said it in Latin. Obscurum per obscurius, ignotum per ignotius.

People. Sergio or Wendy or whatever. Some One Name People go by their surnames, but they are still only One Name People. If you say "Pomeranski and I had lunch", he appears in your mind's eye. But Hirskill Fischmascher was so strange it took two names to catch him in your brain.

He appears. HIRSKILL FISCHMASCHER, like everyone else who is not BILLY is in actuality a slightly grotesque puppet. Operated by the actor playing BILLY.

I hardly spoke to Hirskill Fischmascher. No one spoke to Hirskill Fischmascher except Hirskill Fischmascher. Every recess, he would wander alone, muttering to himself. Most weird kids at Wanlend Heights got the crap pummeled out of them at least once a day, but not even Boker Tunkman was brave enough to beat up Hirskill Fischmascher. Hirskill Fischmascher was way too creepy.

I approached him during a wet, morning recess, four days before my sleepover.

HIRSKILL FISCHMASCHER: *(Mumbling.) Yay ng nga Yog Sothoth.*

BILLY: *Hi.*

HIRSKILL FISCHMASCHER: *Ya, hi.*

BILLY: *I'll invite you t'my birthday if y'do me a favour.*

HIRSKILL FISCHMASCHER: *What sorta favour?*

BILLY: *Oh... Just a favour.*

HIRSKILL FISCHMASCHER: *Does it have anything t'do with the monsters around you?*

BILLY: *How did you know?*

HIRSKILL FISCHMASCHER: *Yer one of those purple aura people. You guys always have monsters around you.*[6]

BILLY: *Yeah. It's got something t'do with that.*

HIRSKILL FISCHMASCHER stares at him. BILLY tries to laugh courageously.

Hechee!

HIRSKILL FISCHMASCHER: *Kay, I'll help you. But only if you promise t'be my Best Friend.*

BILLY: The price was high but my need was desperate.

Kay.

On the way home from school that day, Boker Tunkman and Sander Poochila yelled names at me because I was walking home with Hirskill Fischmascher. Hirskill Fischmascher turned around and stared at them. Their faces went white. Sander yelled, "Freak-head!" as they took off, but since he wasn't facing us we decided to ignore it.

Hirskill FISCHMASCHER: *You don't really hafta be my Best Friend if you don't want to.*

BILLY: *It's okay. Those guys are weenies anyway.*

We got home before my parents. I unlocked the door and we left our shoes on the inside mat. Hirskill Fischmascher's shoes stunk like dead cats. I thought of asking him to put them outside, but since I was his Best Friend now I didn't want to hurt his feelings.

[6] I had a psychic great aunt who used to say creepy crap like this. She worked for the Detroit police force finding dead bodies. No one ever wanted to talk to her at family reunions, in case she said something spooky like, "Your aura is green. Some one is going to drop a safe on your head today."

The monster's upstairs.

HIRSKILL FISCHMASCHER twitches his nose like a blood hound.

HIRSKILL FISCHMASCHER: *Holy! You got a cool room! Can I have yer "Battlestar Gallactica" poster?*

BILLY: *Nah, I kinda need it.*

We looked under my bed. I couldn't see anything but dust bunnies and old Kleenex.

HIRSKILL FISCHMASCHER: *Like I thought. Ya got a succubus in there.*

BILLY: *A succubus?*

HIRSKILL FISCHMASCHER: *Ya. Ya better get her out before yer sleepover er she'll eat off everybody's head. I can make a trap if ya have the right things.*

BILLY: We went to work, gathering up the necessary equipment. My mother came home and caught us rooting around in the cupboards. I told her we needed stuff for a science experiment. She was so excited at the thought of me doing homework instead of playing Atari, she left us alone.

Hirskill Fischmascher put a metal waste basket next to the bed. He dropped a pat of butter into it, then he poured some red Kool-aid around the butter. He lit a match and stuck it, flame up, into the butter, like a birthday candle.

HIRSKILL FISCHMASCHER: *Get ready.*

BILLY: I remember every detail of what happened next. The succubus had a beautiful face. More beautiful than Catwoman's[77] even, except she had fangs

[7] That's Julie Newmar as Catwoman, not Lee Merriweather nor Eartha Kitt.

instead of teeth. Most frightening of all, she was totally, totally bare naked! I mean, you could see everything!!

A screeching is heard.

HIRSKILL FISCHMASCHER: I R'lyeh Cthulhu f'tagen! Ia! IA!

The succubus flies through the room, keening.

BILLY: Suddenly, the succubus was vacuumed into the waste basket.

Suitable noises.

I slammed an Eaton's catalogue over the opening, and Hirskill Fischmascher sealed it with a whole roll of sticky tape.

HIRSKILL FISCHMASCHER: *We should bury it by the creek, so the demoness can never escape.*

BILLY: *Nah. When I'm a teenager, I might want a bare naked woman living under my bed again.*

Then we went downstairs and played with my Micronaughts till it was time for him to go. By the time he left, my mother had put foot powder in his shoes to stop the stink.[8]

Scene II

BILLY: The stupid thing was, I didn't even end up having a sleepover. My Mom took Hirskill Fischmascher and I to the circus instead.

(Singing.)

The circus is a happy place
Full of things unique:

[8] My mother used to do this to a friend named Adam Collier, now forever immortalized as the inspiration for Hirskill Fischmascher's stinky feet.

You can see some pinheads there
And countless other freaks.

They have a man who's just a head
He juggles with his nose.
His wife was born with missing arms
She plays banjo with her toes.

They have a baby bearded girl
And a human fish
Oh, the circus is the happiest place
That you could ever wish.

But there's one thing at the circus
That's unnatural and weird
There is one thing at the circus
Every boy and girl should fear.

His lips are blue
His eyes are wild
His nose is bloody red
He cackles like a psychopath
His skin's so white,
He must be dead!
Beware!
Beware of the clown!

He'll put confetti in your panties
Or he'll bind you with balloons.
He'll crawl into your nightmares
Wearing baggy pantaloons.

The clown might try to kiss you
Or make you squeeze his nose.
The clown might try to squirt you
When you smell his big red rose.

His lips are blue
His eyes are wild
His nose is bloody red
He cackles like a psychopath
His skin's so white,

He must be dead!
Beware!
Beware of the clown!

Scene III

For Hirskill Fischmascher's tenth birthday I bought him the coolest thing ever: a Slave One Space Fighter to go with his Boba Fett action figure. It had these fins that rotated when you pumped this trigger, and Boba Fett could sit inside, and, best of all, it came with a little plastic Han Solo Encased In Carbonite!! Everybody I knew wanted a Slave One, but they were really hard to find, and I figured if Hirskill Fischmascher owned one, maybe it would make him more popular and I wouldn't get beat up so much for hanging out with him.[9]

HIRSKILL FISCHMASCHER: *Thanks Billy! Next time we play "Star Wars" I can have Yoda ride in this!*

BILLY: *It's Boba Fett's ship, you weiner!*

We went down to the creek to play with our figures. The only space ship I owned was an x-wing. Hirskill Fischmascher insisted on Yoda driving the Slave One. So, I had to have my Darth Vader drive the x-wing, otherwise we wouldn't be able to fight each other.

It's stupid having Vader drive an x-wing.

HIRSKILL FISCHMASCHER: *Why?*

BILLY: It was his birthday so I gave in. All the way down to the creek he kept rotating the Slave One's fins

[9] Marc Downing, the composer of *Billy Wuthergloom* and the original Creepy Musician was the only kid I knew who owned a Slave One. I asked him to help with Billy in the hopes he would let me play with it.

and making retarded noises like it was an airplane not a space ship.

Demonstrates.

There was a bunch of grade eights standing where we liked to play. They were smoking cigarettes and flicking the ashes into the water. One of them was Dillinger MacReedy. He was under suspension for showing up drunk at a school dance and barfing on Mrs Rastow's breasts.

Let's play somewhere else.

HIRSKILL FISCHMASCHER: *Naw, I want to play here.*

HIRSKILL runs around with the Slave One over his head, making retarded airplane noises. DILLINGER MACREEDY turns.

DILL: *Hey! Look at the two fags! Have the two little fags come down to the creek to play with each other's boners? Eh, little fags?*

HIRSKILL FISCHMASCHER: *Leave us alone, you weenie!*

DILLINGER begins to beat on HIRSKILL FISCHMASCHER.

BILLY: *Leave him alone.*

DILL: *You want some too, fag?*

BILLY: *No thank you.*

I ran away. The last thing I saw before I rounded the path into the safety of the forest was Dillinger MacReedy yanking the Slave One out of Hirskill Fischmascher's hands and whacking it into the water with a stick.

I could hear Hirskill Fischmascher squealing like a girl.

other stuff too, but I don't want to tell you. It's dirty.

BILLY: The ghost lady's eyes devoured Hirskill Fischmascher.

Let's go. This is freaky.

He wouldn't move. They just stared longingly at each other. A dead lady was bad enough, but now she was doing make-out eyes with my Best Friend!

I grabbed him and pulled him away from the creek.

Horrible double screech.

The lady sank back into the water, a look of unimaginable suffering twisting her face.

Silence.

HIRSKILL FISCHMASCHER: *When I grow up, I'm going to marry that lady. She's beautiful.*

BILLY: I should have known right then that someday I would be without him.

Scene IV

We were lily white and innocent
Before the necromancy came
Except for cross bars on our bicycles,
Girls and boys were just the same.

We had the same flat nipples
And we were only 3 foot 3,
And our tiny hairless genitals
Were just things we used to pee.

But while we slept like Winkens and Blinkens and Noddies
Lascivious Spirits crept into our bodies
Demons, obscene and nefarious

Crawled into the bones, skin and hair of us,
Friends that I knew to be pristine and true
Grew strange and started to change.

Brig Bodrug was the first they took
The first one of us to fall
He laughed out loud one gym class
When the coach cried, "Pick up all your balls."

Elisa Po was next to go
The demons came to get her.
Two tiny lumps sprouted on her chest
Which she hid beneath her sweater.

Maria Hogg[10] *was fine till spring*
Then the curse for her did come.
Its crimson, hell-sent harbinger,
A red splotch on the seat of her bum.

Anthony Tang was the next they claimed.
He asked to pee one day
We found him in the Boys' Room
Reading a catalogue from the Bay.

The demons took them, one by one,
And made them rank with Hosts of Hell,
All at once a foul effluvia
From their underarms did smell.

But while we slept like Winkens and Blinkens and Noddies
Lascivious Spirits crept into our bodies
Demons, obscene and nefarious
Crawled into the bones, skin and hair of us,
Friends that I knew to be pristine and true
Grew strange and started to change.

[10] When naming the unseen children in *Billy Wuthergloom,* I developed the dangerous habit of using the first name of one person I knew in public school and smooshing it together with the last name of another. So if, for example, I knew you in grade three and your first name is Maria, or your last name is Hogg and you're reading this now, then you probably have every right to be suspicious.

They've all changed, those kids I knew,
Through black diabolly
And one day soon, I fear, I pray,
The demons will come for me.

BILLY: At the age of twelve I had my first wet dream. I was on a wildly undulating roller coaster, holding hands with Sabrina Newmeyer[11]. The jerk of a sudden curve jostled our position so that her fingers were resting gently on my thing. My pants magically melted away and, instead of my hand, she was holding my thing as it got harder. And she didn't seem to notice! We were climbing a very steep slope that went on and on. We reached the summit and were suspended in space for an instant. Sabrina looked down, saw my thing in her hand, and started to scream! We plunged down the precipitous drop! The car lifted off the rails and I tumbled into a deep wet hole. I landed on top of the Succubus from under my bed. Her legs were wrapped around me. "Welcome down here!" she said. And she licked my neck and I exploded. When I woke up I was covered in sticky white goo. For a full eighteen hours I thought I had a disease till I discovered a dusty family medical encyclopedia with a paragraph on "nocturnal emissions".

Sabrina Newmeyer was my girl friend. Sabrina's Best Friend, Trina, sent me a note one day that said," Do you like Sabrina? Yes. Maybe. Only sort of." I checked the box that said "Maybe" and passed it back to Trina and that's how Sabrina and I started going out. Except her mother wouldn't let her date until her sixteenth birthday. So she said I could hold her hand, and sit with her on the school bus, but we couldn't kiss or anything because that would constitute dating. I agreed because why would I want to go kissing anybody?

[11] Of course, some of the names I just made up.

After the dream, in bed, with the white goop all over me, I got to thinking about the naked succubus and I wondered if maybe it might be fun to look at her again because...well, I didn't really know why, but I was curious about her boobs because Sabrina was starting to grow some.

He opens the SUCCUBUS's cage and she comes flying out into the air.

SUCCUBUS: I'm going to suck your bones!

She disappears.

BILLY: *Oops.*

Hirskill Fischmascher hadn't been to school much lately. A doctor told his mother that he had a mental illness. So she kept putting him in the loony bin.

The morning after my...nocturnal emission, he phoned me from a pay phone.

HIRSKILL FISCHMASCHER: *Hi, are you okay? I have a bad feeling. You didn't summon any dark spirits did you?*

BILLY: *...I donno.*

HIRSKILL FISCHMASCHER: Look, don't worry cuz the doctor says I can go to school an' stuff starting on Monday, so I'll be around to look out fer ya. Spread salt on your window ledge though, 'kay?

BILLY: *Sure.*

HIRSKILL FISCHMASCHER: *Smell ya later!*

BILLY: At recess that day I was musing on my relationship with Sabrina. Just holding hands was okay, but maybe I was missing out on...stuff. My mind started to wander. Soon I was pretending I was Jabba the Hutt and Sabrina Newmeyer was Princess Leia on a chain in her little bikini outfit.[12]

A cold finger stroked my neck.

Whirls around and finds himself face to face with SABRINA.

Sabrina!

I had a wild thought she could tell I'd been thinking dirty things about her!

SABRINA: *My mother said it was okay for me to have a Hallowe'en party and the whole class can come. But I want some time with you alone. 'Kay Punkin?*

BILLY: *Ah... Sure. Yeah, sure. Wait... Uh... Can Hirskill Fischmascher come too?*

SABRINA: *You mean the Loony? Why not. It's Hallowe'en.*

She laughs flirtatiously and disappears.

BILLY: I was mad that she'd called Hirskill Fischmascher a Loony, but at least she'd said he could come to the party.

BILLY and HIRSKILL FISCHMASCHER get ready for the party. BILLY is dressed as a scary clown. HIRSKILL FISCHMASCHER is dressed as a one-eyed Viking god of the dead.

Everybody in all of grade seven was there. We had the whole house for the party except the upstairs was out of bounds. People danced to *Thriller* in the basement. And watched *Children of the Corn* in the living room. And talked in the kitchen. A few people went into the dining room to sit under the table and neck.

[12] At this very moment in movie history, while watching *Return of the Jedi*, my entire generation hit puberty. Puberty ended several years later, as Sherilyn Fenn tied her cherry stem in a knot with her mouth on *Twin Peaks*.

I hung out with Hirskill Fischmascher.

Sabrina was dressed as Isis and her costume consisted of almost nothing with some snake shaped jewelry on her wrists and ankles! She was acting weird and it bothered me. But it made me feel kind of tickly too.

HIRSKILL FISCHMASCHER: *I gotta go pee.*

Exits. SABRINA slinks over to BILLY.

SABRINA: *Billy*, will you come upstairs with me?

BILLY: She lead me up to her forbidden bedroom and shut the door behind us. I suspected she was about to do something sexy, but whether that was desirable or horrific I couldn't decide.

They stare awkwardly at one another for a long while. BILLY forces a big smile. She kisses his forehead. Then his cheek. Then his nose. Then his lips. Then his lips again.[13]

Then she put her tongue in my mouth. At first I didn't know what it was. I just felt this big wet thing flopping around in there. Then I realized I was chickening out on my first ever kiss, so I closed my eyes and offered up my mouth for her to smooch.

Closes eyes. She pushes him down to a prone position.

I couldn't decide if I liked it or not. It was like chewing gum that chewed back.

After a while I got bored and opened my eyes to peek. Only then did I realize the unearthly danger I was in!

[13] The original Sabrina puppet was the head of a toilet plunger with big blue eyes sprouting from the top. If you use a similar puppet, you can expect a very big laugh here. If your puppet isn't a plunger head, well, you're on your own.

SABRINA has transformed into the SUCCUBUS! O Horror!

SUCCUBUS: *I'm going to suck your bones!*

BILLY: *HELP! HIRSKILL FISCHMASCHER, SAVE ME!!*

HIRSKILL FISCHMASCHER appears.

HIRSKILL FISCHMASCHER: What's goin' on?

BILLY: *The succubus! From under my bed! I let her out! Now she's Sabrina! Sabrina is trying to eat me up! She's the succubus!*

But SABRINA is herself again.

SABRINA: *Billy, you are such a weiner! Why don't you french with your boyfriend here!*

She exits.

HIRSKILL FISCHMASCHER: *I think you just did something real stupid.*

BILLY: *Yeah. Sorry. I should have tol' you I let the succubus out.*

HIRSKILL FISCHMASCHER: *Nah. I mean when you kiss a girl you should keep your eyes closed so that doesn't happen.*

BILLY: I went downstairs to apologize, but Sabrina was under the dining room table, necking with Sander Poochila. That made me sad, but I got over it.

Scene V

(Singing.)

Howl! Howl! The Devil has claimed me!
Howl! Howl! I'm a lycanthrope now!

Howl! Howl! My passion ensnares me!
Howl! Howl! Howl!

When Danny Skink was just a child
He was pure of spirit, meek and mild.
He was his parents' pride and joy,
When Danny Skink was just a boy.
But horror struck when he turned twelf
And Dan began to touch himself.

When Laura Lodge[14] *was walking by*
Her skirt blew up and showed her thigh.
So stunning was the virgin flesh,
Dan closed his eyes and saw it fresh.
The moon was full, the hour late
When Dan began to masturbate.

But tragic horror stopped not there
His sweaty palms were sprouting hair!
He stroked an onanistic flurry.
His nose grew long, his face grew furry.
As pressure down inside increased,
Dan transformed from Boy to Beast.

He cried:
Howl! Howl! The Devil has claimed me!
Howl! Howl! I'm a lycanthrope now!
Howl! Howl! My passion ensnares me!
Howl! Howl! Howl!

The little death at last did burst
But Dan had changed from bad to worst.
The sticky goo, like from a foamy gulf
Found Dan a snarling demi-wulf
Who drooled and barked and growled and cussed
And felt no other drive but lust!

[14] I went to school with this girl named Jennifer Lodge (whose best friend was named Laura Erskine) and I really hadn't seen her since we were 13. So, she's 31 now and she and her husband happen to stumble into a performance of *Billy Wuthergloom* in London, Ontario, having no idea what to expect. Now, imagine you're her husband; Are you disturbed at this moment? Or are you happy that you have married a woman who has inspired art?

At that horrid instant, Dan's Dad burst in
And saw a wolf where his son had been.
He took a knife, with silver tempered,
And chopped off Dan's offending member.
And with no genitals to make him sin,
He transformed from Beast to Boy again.

He cries:
Howl! Howl! The Devil forsakes me!
Howl! Howl! I'm a eunuch boy now!
Howl! Howl! My passion escapes me!
Howl! Howl! Howl!

Scene VI

BILLY: When I was in grade nine, the cool thing to do was head down to the Gomorrah Plaza Mall food court and skip our afternoon classes. At least, that was what the older kids did, so we did too. We being me and Sander Poochila, and Boker Tunkman. I didn't really like Sander or Boker, but they were the only guys in all of Barkingdark High School that I ever hung out with. Hirskill Fischmascher didn't go to Barkingdark. His mother sent him to a high school for kids who were crazy.

Sander and Boker liked the Mall because they could shop-lift from the record stores but I kept going down with them anyway, because Sherry McGinnis was usually there , and I liked to look at her. She was in grade twelve, a whole three years older than I was, and that made her as unreachable as Cleopatra, but I dreamed about her every day. And all night. Most of the girls in my grade said she was a bitch, but I think they were just jealous because Sherry was so much prettier than they were.

It was well known she only dated jerks—druggies with rich parents who bragged about doing her. I think most of them made it up. To me she was a tragic heroine, like Kim Basinger in *9 1/2 Weeks.*[15] And man! Did I wanna have sex with her in front of a fridge!

One Wednesday in April, I was sitting in the food court alone, trying to excavate some ice from the bottom of an empty cup with a straw. Sherry was a few tables away, eating sadly by herself.

She felt my eyes on her and looked up. I fought the impulse to jerk my head away. I smiled a smile that I hoped was friendly and yet sexually provocative at the same time.

He does.

My lips felt like I'd borrowed them from somebody else's face. Sherry's eyes glimmered and then she smiled!

HIRSKILL FISCHMASCHER: *Hiya Billy!*

BILLY: Sherry McGinnis was smiling at ME! Me! A lowly niner with no friends except two little hoods! And Hirskill Fischmascher had to crawl out from under his rock and wreck it!

Get lost! Ya stinkin' loony!

Hirskill Fischmascher's eyes filled up with wet hurt. Then he left. I wanted to call after him. I turned back to Sherry's table. She was gone too!

I sprang from my seat and raced off to find her. Hirskill Fischmascher always said Gomorrah Plaza Mall was a twisted labyrinth, because the guy who designed it was plagued by devils.

[15] Those of you paying very close attention, who also happen to have encyclopedic knowledge of dates and pop culture, might have noticed that it is impossible for Billy to be in grade nine, and to have seen *9 1/2 Weeks*, given that it didn't come out until the following year. However, take my word for it, you are the first person who ever noticed.

He gets lost in the mall.

I stopped in front of a Body Shop outlet to get my bearings. With Sherry lost, maybe I should find Hirskill Fischmascher and apologize. But I had no idea which way I'd come. Besides I really had to pee.

As I entered the john, my reflection in the mirror glared at me with contempt.

He shudders. Steps up to a urinal and pees.

Then I thought I glimpsed the succubus from the corner of my eye! I looked back at the mirror, and my reflection was gone. I stood on my tip toes to see if it was ducking behind the reflection of the counter. No. Nor was it hiding in any of the reflected stalls. I checked the real stalls. I even looked in the toilet bowls. No reflection! I fled back to Barkingdark Highschool.

Not having a reflection is more disconcerting than you might think. First there are the obvious problems: Is there peanut butter on my face? Boogers in my nose? Is my hair a mess?

He wipes his face.

Worse, was a creeping feeling that I didn't really exist. Maybe it wasn't my reflection that had run off, but my real self. Hirskill Fischmascher stopped calling me. And I felt like too much of a dink to call him. Sherry was rumoured to have found a new boyfriend, and everyone said he was amazing. I wanted to lay down under a bus.

One Friday night, three weeks after my reflection escaped, I took walk along the strip of Solomon Road that had all the university patio bars. Sometimes the older kids at Barkingdark High would sneak in with fake I.D. I hoped I'd catch a glimpse of Sherry McGinnis in the arms of this new beau, so I'd have the pleasure of wallowing in even deeper self pity. As I passed the patio bars some frat boys called after me, "Heya Heathcliff!"

(To himself.) Heathcliff?

I just kept walking.

My brain didn't know where I was going, but my feet seemed to be following some special calling. I turned down a side street and found myself in the train station parking lot. There was this grey Oldsmobile. For some reason, I strutted over to it, opened the passenger door and got inside. The whole time I was thinking, "Stop! Hand, don't open that door! Stop it bum! Don't sit in that seat!" But my body parts weren't listening to me.

There was someone sitting behind the wheel. It was Sherry McGinnis!

SHERRY: *You're early.*

BILLY: Like she expected me! Then she leaned over and gave me a kiss! Her mouth was open so I put my tongue in it. She didn't pull away! She even made this kind of purring noise! She reached up my shirt and then reached through the hole to stroke my chest! Since she was touching my chest, maybe I could touch hers too. As I reached towards her, she actually slipped my hand under her bra so I was actually touching her bare naked breast! Holy moly!

SHERRY: *My Mom says I can have the car till twelve thirty, and I found the perfect place to park. I want our first time to be perfect. I love you so much, Heathcliff! No guy has ever treated me so, you know, like a person before.*

BILLY: And then she kissed me again, and, with our tongues all tied up, I couldn't think of a tactful way to tell her my name wasn't Heathcliff.

SHERRY: *Let's go.*

BILLY: *Okay.*

SHERRY: *Do you have the things?*

BILLY: *...The things?*

SHERRY: *The things.*

BILLY: *...Oh! The—those—the...I forgot... Uh. Do we need... Right we should. Just. There's a drugstore right—I'll be right— Don't leave.*

I'd never bought things before, but I knew what brands to avoid. Trojans were out, because they were named after these little guys who sneaked into a town by slipping out of a big horse. Ramses was the name of the pharaoh in the Ten Commandments who let all the little Hebrews escape through the parted Red Sea. Durex is just a stupid name. I figured I'd go with Sheik. Sheik reminded me of that Valentino guy from the old movies and he was supposed to be sexy. But I never got to the drugstore.

There, right in front of me, was my reflection! His hair was spiked and his clothes were really cool, like Adam Ant. At first I didn't recognize him as me, that's how cool he looked.

BILLY's REFLECTION: *Keep your hands off my girl!*

BILLY: *You're Heathcliff?*

The REFLECTION punches BILLY in the mouth. BILLY falls to the REFLECTION's feet.

Even his boots were cooler than mine!

BILLY is kicked.

After that I was pretty much unconscious.

When I woke up, I phoned Hirskill Fischmascher. He was still mad, and it took a long time to convince him to help me. I had to apologize five times and promise to give him my *X-men* comics. Then I took the bus over to his house. His mother was downstairs, drinking with her boyfriend. We went upstairs to his room. He had this big mirror leaning against the wall and some orange juice and dirt in a bowl with leaves floating in it. I looked into the mirror, and saw everything in it, except me.

HIRSKILL FISCHMASCHER: *Wow! You're worse off than I thought.*

BILLY: He threw some of the orange juice and leaves on me, and the image in the mirror changed. Instead of Hirskill Fischmascher's bedroom it showed a graveyard with an Oldsmobile parked in it. And inside the Oldsmobile, my reflection and Sherry McGinnis were going at it! They were both totally naked. They weren't actually doing it yet, but they were doing things that looked like a lot of fun. Things I'd never even thought of.

HIRSKILL FISCHMASCHER: Ia Shub Niggurath!

BILLY: The graveyard and car and sex stuff faded away. In their place stood my reflection staring back at me. He didn't look so cool any more, he just looked like me, only really pissed off. I guess if I was about to have sex with Sherry McGinnis and then had to go back to staring at me, I might not be so happy either.

BILLY's REFLECTION: *Beware Wuthergloom! She gets closer each night!*

BILLY: Then he went back to mirroring my every movement like a reflection should.

(To HIRSKILL.) Thanks... I'm, like, sorry I called you a loony and all that.

HIRSKILL FISCHMASCHER: *That's okay. It must be tough having a nut bar for your best friend.*

Scene VII

(Singing.)

Jack was dating Erin Hetrick[16]
For 'bout seven months or so.
She didn't really like him
As far as boyfriends go.
She'd take a fierce exception
To near every word he said.
But Jack said she would fool around
And sometimes give him head.

They'd fight with fierce abandon
And square off face to face.
But before the night had ended,
They'd be locked in an embrace.
One day in grade twelve gym class,
Jack said they'd go all the way
When his folks left town that weekend.
This was all that I could say:

Don't lose your virginity, Jack.
The flesh is crawling up my back.
It's not time for an ejac-
Ulation. Copulation is an error.
This girl fills me up with terror.
Don't lose your virginity, Jack!

Jack scoffed and called me chicken
Cuz I feared his big first night.
But I quaked with trepidation.
Something didn't feel quite right.
That Friday they were naked
And there was no chaperon,

[16] This name is also an amalgam. However, after the Jennifer Lodge incident, I am reluctant to name the sources or why I chose them.

So they slipped up to the bedroom
To reel the Big Fish home.

In a minute it was over.
Jack was out where he'd been in.
Then Erin started hissing
And she peeled right off her skin.
She tore off her human outsides
And was serpentine beneath.
She wrapped her coils around him
And she flashed her poison teeth.

Don't lose your virginity, Jack.
The flesh is crawling up my back.
It's not time for an ejac-
Ulation. Copulation is an error.
This girl fills me up with terror.
Don't lose your virginity, Jack!

She swallowed him, one single gulp,
He had hardly time to scream.
She put her outsides on again.
You couldn't see the seam.
But her belly bulged a little
Where poor Jack was trapped inside.
By the time she'd done digesting,
I guess poor Jack had died.

Jack tried to be a studhorse
Now he's hamburger instead.
I tried my best to warn him
But now he's gone and dead.
But at least he's not a virgin.
Now I know what I must do.
I don't want to be a loser,
So I must have sex too.

Don't lose your virginity, Jack.
The flesh is crawling up my back.
It's not time for an ejac-
Ulation. Copulation is an error.

This girl fills me up with terror.
Don't lose your virginity, Jack!

Scene VIII

BILLY: This story is the saddest thing that ever happened to me. It happened during May Two-Four weekend the year after I graduated from high school.

Hirskill Fischmascher had been missing for three years and he'd just come back out of the blue. Everyone but me thought he was dead. But I always figured if Hirskill Fischmascher was dead his ghost would have come to say goodbye. We had that kind of bond. He'd been living out on the street. I'm not going to say anything more, because I get terrible pictures in my head when I think about the horrible things that happened to him.

HIRSKILL FISCHMASCHER: *I'm so tired, Billy. I think I'm going to going to marry her soon.*

BILLY: Whatter you talking about, doofus?

HIRSKILL FISCHMASCHER: *I'm so tired.*

BILLY: We were standing on the dock of my girlfriend's cottage.

Her name was Ruthy Grahame. We met in grade 13 during our school's production of *Oklahoma*. At first, I wasn't going to audition because Sander Poochila and Boker Tunkman kept calling it Oklahomo. But I tried out anyway and I got Will Parker and Ruthy was Ado Annie.

Before she went out with me, she had sex with Sander Poochila. Sander was a real weenie to her though. He was secretly sleeping with Kelly

Masters too, and when Ruthy found out she was really cut up about it. She didn't want to have sex with me right away because of what happened with Sander. I said I understood, but really it bugged me, because, she was, like experienced, and I hadn't been with anybody but myself.

We did try to have sex once, the day of our grad. But it was a disaster. First, when Ruthy was all naked, I started to think how much she looked like the succubus. Then, I had like, condom trouble. I don't care how many times you practice for this moment, the first time you try to put a condom on in action, it's just not the same. You feel rushed. You put it on inside out and have to take it off again. Then it doesn't unroll right. Then, maybe you lose your erection a little, maybe. And after that, it doesn't fit properly. Like, you got too much air in it. I felt like I was wearing a giant rubber sock.

I couldn't get anything to, you know, work. Ruthy started to giggle and I just gave up.[17]

Anyway, Ruthy was totally smart, so she got this great scholarship and moved away to take this double major in drama and sociology. My marks weren't good enough to get into university, so I stayed at home and took this crappy job making doughnuts until I could find myself. We were trying to have a long distance relationship. Things weren't going well because she was meeting all these great university guys. I wasn't meeting anybody because wherever I went I smelled like doughnuts.

Her parents had this cottage up north, and May Two-Four weekend she had this party at it. She said I could invite Hirskill Fischmascher so it wouldn't be just me and a bunch of her university

[17] Sometimes, people ask me how much of *Billy Wuthergloom* is autobiographical. I usually try to avoid answering.

friends. That's why Hirskill Fischmascher was there in the first place.

It was early evening, and already I was pretty drunk. Hirskill Fischmascher was sober because booze screwed up his medication. Ruthy was supposed to be bringing me a drink. But twenty minutes had gone by, and I was starting to think she was deliberately dawdling to piss me off.

A car honked its horn. I heard Ruthy squeal happily.

I gotta go check something.

Hirskill Fischmascher smiled at me like I wasn't being a self-centred asshole at all.

In front of the cottage was a flashy red Camaro. Standing beside it was this tall, handsome university guy. Ruthy was giving him a big hug.

Hey! What's going on?

RUTHY: *Oh, Bill. I want you to meet Dillinger. He's my TA.*

DILL: *Nice to meet you, Chief.*

BILLY: *We've met.*

DILL: *...Sorry, Chief. I don't seem to recall.*

BILLY: *Forget it.*

I stomped off to get another beer. Later on, we were all sitting around a camp fire and all the smoke was blowing in my face. The conversation was totally highbrow, and it was making me feel like a grade A dickhead.

RUTHY: *But surely you agree society is losing its ability to put information in context. We may have greater access to all these factoids, but we're incapable of seeing how any of them connect.*

DILL: *You're only saying that because you have an interest in quote unquote Theatre. Have you seen the film "My Dinner with Andre"? A character says that acting is just people doing a bad imitation of real life. That really clicked for me. I see more exciting drama in the pub every Thursday night.*[18]

HIRSKILL FISCHMASCHER: *An actor in a movie said there was no point to watching acting? And you believed him?*

Pause.

DILL: *Did I ask you, you fucking wacko?*

BILLY: Something snapped inside of me, and suddenly I was ten years old again, standing on the edge of the creek. I leapt across the campfire and buried my fists in Dillinger MacReedy's smug face. He cracked me so hard on the nose that I thought my eyes were going to fly out of my head.

DILL: *It was a joke, you asshole!*

RUTHY: *Billy, I never want to see you again!*

BILLY: I heard the splash at the same time as everyone else. But, for me, it was the only sound in the world. I leapt to my feet and ran down towards the dock.

Here's what everyone else told the police they saw happen: Hirskill Fischmascher slipped away during the fight. He ran to the end of the dock, jumped in the water and started to sink. I swam out after him, but I didn't make it in time. He drowned. Everyone figured he committed suicide because he was just a loony and what Dillinger said made him lose it.

This is what I saw:

[18] Some guy really said this to me, only he said "Dinner with Andrew" and he pronounced in "Thee-Ay-tur".

I saw Hirskill dog paddle out into the lake. He was heading towards the dead lady from the creek, who had risen out of the water and was calling him. I swam after him, but not to save him. I swam out because I was afraid of Hirskill Fischmascher leaving me alone. When I reached them, the dead lady and Hirskill were locked in a tight embrace, their lips sharing a sensual kiss.

I decided, quite calmly, to let myself drown. I slipped under the surface. In the dark water I felt Hirskill's hands around me, buoying me up. He didn't seem to be swimming; he was gliding through the water. He hoisted me onto the dock, and pressed something into my hands. The next moment he was standing in the middle of the lake, his pasty skin silver in the moonlight. The dead lady held his left hand, and with his right hand he waved to me, goodbye.

Hirskill, please don't go!

Then they were gone.

I looked down at his parting gift. It was a little plastic Han Solo Encased in Carbonite.

At Hirskill Fischmascher's funeral, I told Ruthy I'd try really hard not to be jealous of her university life. Ruthy said she loved me enough to give me a second chance and after that we had sex. I was still kinda crappy at it. But I figured sex was something that took practice. And you know what? She didn't look like a succubus once the whole time we were doing it.

And she never told me off for the rock I'd put through the window of Dillinger MacReedy's Camaro either, the night my Best Friend, Hirskill, married his life-long love and disappeared from this world forever.

Sometimes I'm lonely without him.

Scene IX

(Singing.)

Goodnight ladies; goodnight men.
It's time to step into darkness again.
Tonight when you're nestled in bed with your mate,
Your love-making's finished, and it's become late,
And your eyes start to struggle to peer through the black.
You can't see your lover. She can't see you back.
Then terror's ignited from this tiny spark
About all the things you can't see in the dark.
The body beside you who's sharing your bed
Might be reaching to kill you, or maybe she's dead.
She maybe has fangs and could bite out your heart.
How can you know in this terrible dark?
But horror is pointless, there's nowhere to run.
Darkness is everywhere under the sun.
Horror is pointless, there's nowhere to run.
Darkness is everywhere under the sun.
It's dark in the hallway, the kitchen is too.
It's dark in the bathroom when you go to poo.
It's dark in the basement. The laundry room's dark.
It's dark in the street. It's dark in the park.
All of the city is dark as can be.
Dark, the whole province. Dark the country.
All the grim Earth is in darkness at night.
So take my advice and sleep with a light.

So take my advice and sleep with a light.

The End.

Grendelmaus

Set and Characters

The set is simple and expressionistic, able to represent multiple locations in and around the city of New Bosford with as little shuffling around as possible. It consists of a few platforms, a chair or two and a screen behind which the actors can enter, exit and stash unused puppets. The screen should also double as the Punch and Judy puppet theatre.[1]

There are two actors, one plays Ishmael, and the other plays Rachel. The remaining characters are puppets, operating by the actors, in full view of the audience. No attempt is made to hide the performers, save in the instance of the hand puppets used in the prologue and Scene XIII and IX.

The Actor playing Ishmael operates:

-the hand puppets

-Grendelmaus

-Bildad

-Waiter

-Clerk

-Old Man

-Mr Fedallah

The Actor playing Rachel operates:

-Mrs Coffin

-Mrs Stubb

-Djinn

-Starbuck

Some puppets require two operators. The above indicates which puppeteer is principally responsible for voice and characterization.

The events depicted are based on a true story.

[1] But as it didn't in the original production, it doesn't really have to in yours.

Production Information

Grendelmaus premiered on June 6, 2002, at the Berkley Street Upstairs Theatre, Toronto, with the following cast:

ISHMAEL .... Eric Woolfe
RACHEL .... Mary Frances Moore

Directed by Michael Waller
Designed by Joanne Dente
Lighting design by Rick Banville
Puppets by Eric Woolfe
Necromantic Administration by Samara Nicholds
Stage Manager: Tamerrah Volkovskis

Prologue

The preshow music ends with "An Indoor Sea Shanty."[2] *From the darkness we hear a female voice chant out...*

RACHEL's VOICE: Hwaet! We Gar-Dena in geAr-dagum
theod-cyninga thrym gefrunon
Hu tha aethelingas ellen fremedon![3]

Lights up on a traditional Punch and Judy stage. RACHEL is sitting beside it, on a stool.

RACHEL: Once upon a time, when the world was dark, and monsters roamed freely, there lived a happy king, named King Hrothgar, Lord of the Scyldings.

Enter HROTHGAR.

HROTHGAR: Hello, everyone! Hello! It's my birthday today and you're all invited to my place for pig flesh and mead!

Enter GUY 1.

GUY 1: Pig flesh and mead? That's my favourite.

HROTHGAR: Well, there's plenty for everybody.

HROTHGAR exits.

GUY 1: Hey! Bill! Party at the King's place! He's serving pig flesh and mead!

[2] Available on *The Strange and Eerie Soundtrack of Billy Wuthergloom* (Copyright Woolfe and Downing, 2000).
[3] The first lines of *Beowulf*. They mean "So. The Spear-Danes in days gone by/ and the kings who rules them had courage and greatness./ We have heard of those princes' heroic campaigns." Admittedly, it sounds more austere in Old English.

Enter GUY 2. GUY 1 wanders off for a moment.

GUY 2: Pig flesh and mead! Huzzah! I can't wait!

Enter HROTHGAR, with pig flesh and mead.

HROTHGAR: Here you go! Drink up! Be merry!

He exits.

GUY 2: Yummy! Mmmm! Hurry up Bill, this is great!

GUY 1: Hey Bill! Save some for me!

RACHEL: King Hrothgar's party guests, the Brave Brothers Bill, ate and drank until their bellies were so full there was nothing left to do but sleep and belch.

GUY 1: G'night, Bill.

GUY 2: Sleep tight, Bill.

RACHEL: But then a terrible thing happened! An evil ogre named Grendel wandered in from the godless Fens and feasted upon the sleeping revelers.

Grendel enters.

GRENDEL: Da com of more under mist-hleothum
Grendel gongan Godes yrre baer![4]

He eats the guests up. There are limbs and blood everywhere.

Mm. Pig flesh and mead. My favourite.

GRENDEL exits. HROTHGAR enters.

HROTHGAR: O my! O me! My guests have been eaten! That's going to look bad when I come up for re-election![5]

[4] Also from *Beowulf*. It means, "In off the moors, down through the mist bands/ God-cursed Grendel came greedily loping."
[5] Little known fact: The Vikings had an elected council, in which both men and women could vote and elect leaders.

RACHEL: King Hrothgar wept, because the savage thing had invaded his castle in the night, and, after all, a king's castle is his home, and a home invaded isn't so homey anymore.

HROTHGAR: Besides, monsters are creepy.

Enter BEOWULF.

BEOWULF: I'll rid you of the monster!

HROTHGAR: Who are you!

BEOWULF: My name is Beowulf. and without a moment's pause, I'll kill the thing with my bare hands!

HROTHGAR: It's a deal!

HROTHGAR exits.

RACHEL: Beowulf waited in the Hall of Hrothgar for Grendel to return.

GRENDEL enters. They fight. BEOWULF tears off his arm and beats the monster to death. There is blood everywhere.

GRENDEL: My mother's gonna kick your ass!

GRENDEL dies.

BEOWULF: Yes! I rule!

He exits heroically.

RACHEL: Then a strange thing happened. As the fly-caked carcass of Grendel rotted in the Hall of Hrothgar, a small white Mouse stole in.

Flies buzz around the body. A MOUSE enters.

RACHEL: It was the dead of winter, and food was scarce. The poor Mouse was lured in from the deep, white snow by the smell of Grendel's yummy, fresh flowing gore.

MOUSE: Mm! Gore! Yummy!

The MOUSE sniffs. Draws near to the body. and eats of GRENDEL's corpse.

RACHEL: The demon's cursed blood made the Mouse strong and wise, and very powerful. Worst of all, Grendel's blood, which bore the unholy taint of his grandparents, Lillith and Cain, made the Mouse evil, and as cunning as the serpent that spurred the fall of man. From that day on, the Mouse could not die, and he wandered the Earth till the crack of Doom.

Scene I

GRENDELMAUS: *(Off. A scary disembodied voice from the darkness.)*

Da com of more under mist-hleothum
Grendel gongan Godes yrre baer!

Lights up. A dingy bachelor apartment. ISHMAEL is sitting on a couch reading Carl Jung's "An Answer to Job".[6] Something catches ISHMAEL's attention. He sniffs: it's disgusting whatever it is. He looks around. Nothing. He attempts to return to his books, seemingly distraught with the functional nose sitting on his face. Then, a large, ferocious white MOUSE enters. It scampers across the floor. Stops. Stares at ISHMAEL.

ISHMAEL: Oh crap.

Scene II

An office pen. It is dusty, and strewn with ancient office debris which could only be used for some meaningless Sysiphian task. ISHMAEL enters. A

[6] Or the Seamus Heaney translation of *Beowulf*. You pick.

box flies on from the darkness. He catches it.

RACHEL: *(Off.)* Hi.

ISHMAEL: Hi!

A second, large box rockets on. ISHMAEL catches it too.

RACHEL: *(Off.)* New guy.

ISHMAEL: Ya. Um. New guy.

RACHEL: *(Off.)* Condolences.

ISHMAEL: Omigod Rachel Stubb. Right?

RACHEL: *(Off.)* Yeah…

ISHMAEL: Ishmael. From Barkingdark High School.

Finally, RACHEL enters, carrying more boxes. She is a pretty young woman of about thirty. She still has much of the circus about her.

RACHEL: Omigod! Ishmael? Is that you?

ISHMAEL: Omigod!

RACHEL: Omigod!

She jumps up to hug him. He offers his hand and quickly switches to return the embrace. She, in turn, offers her hand. They laugh and finally hug. She breaks first.

ISHMAEL: Wow. You look…wonderful.

RACHEL: You haven't changed at all.

ISHMAEL: Well, lost a bit of hair, I guess.

RACHEL: You'd hardly notice. It looks good on you.

ISHMAEL: Aw, c'mon.

RACHEL: No really. It's right jim.

ISHMAEL: What?

RACHEL: It's, you know, sharpish.

ISHMAEL: You're as pulchritudinous as ever.

RACHEL: Huh?

ISHMAEL: You look really well.

RACHEL: Wow. Wow. Huh. What are you doing here?

ISHMAEL: I don't know really. I have a job title. I'm an Accounts and Internal/External Correspondence Archivist.

RACHEL: Pucky rube. Me too. You're going to die in here.

ISHMAEL: At least we'll be able to catch up. How bad can it be?

RACHEL: It's a muck run. The muckiest. Especially for you, used to open waters. These walls'll stimy you. The air in here is older than me.

ISHMAEL: Last I heard you'd run off with the circus.

RACHEL: Right after we graduated, just like we promised. I was a fly kinker. Lady Armada of The Flying Trapeze, the Pavlova of the Safety Hoop. The advance men used to spiel that my name on a herald as good as guaranteed a turnaway. Are you on shore leave?

ISHMAEL: I'm sorry I missed your act. I always imagined you'd be really good. You—um: you seemed to have picked up the vocational nomenclature without too much difficulty.

RACHEL: The what?

ISHMAEL: Nothing. I bet you were great at it.

RACHEL: I was a rare ducket. But after a while it's hard to tell the bally from the grind. It's exciting when it's some one else's life, but when it's yours, it just, you know, life. Besides, I kept getting my heart finked. Enough about that. How're the seven seas?

ISHMAEL: Um. I never got around to it.

RACHEL: What do you mean? You and I had a pledge. I hit the canvas; you hit the decks. That's what we said. That was one of my comforts while I sit here and rot. I thought you'd be with it.

ISHMAEL: Yes. It—it—it just seemed imprudent, casting off from the land for voluminous stretches. Something always held me back. Sorry. I could still. I plan too.

RACHEL: Well, you were always the clever one. Look at me. I took the leap and my catcher was finked.

ISHMAEL: Sorry?

RACHEL: Forget it. It's a minor disappointment. It'll get lost in the crowd.

Enter BILDAD[7], a puppet.

BILDAD: Mr—Um. Miss Stub are you helping Mr—uh—our new team-member get settled and down to work? Or are you jeopardizing both your employments on his first day?

RACHEL: I am just showing him the layabout, Mr Bildad.

ISHMAEL: She's just—I'm settling right in.

BILDAD: Good. I'm happy to hear you're both getting down to business. The work day is a dangerous thing to waste.

ISHMAEL: Yes it is, Mr Bildad.

[7] All the names are from *Moby Dick,* incidentally. Except those found in the Dirty Hamster monologue later on.

BILDAD: You'll do well here, Mr—um. You'll see he learns the ropes, Miss Stubb. Quickly and efficiently. Or else.

RACHEL: Will do, sir.

BILDAD: Excellent. Excellent.

He exits.

RACHEL: Gaffed-up pickled punk.

ISHMAEL: *(Whispers.)* It's good to see you.

RACHEL: *(Whispers.)* You're an idiot. Get out while you still can.

Scene III

ISHMAEL's apartment. ISHMAEL sniffs inquisitively. MRS COFFIN enters, unseen.

COFFIN: Mr Ishmael, yes. I come you for the rent!

ISHMAEL: Oh, Mrs Coffin! I'm glad to see you. I have a mouse in my apartment.

COFFIN: No pets. You lease is no pets.

ISHMAEL: No. It's not mine. A mouse got in. There is a mouse in my apartment.

COFFIN: Mouse where?

ISHMAEL: On the floor mostly.

COFFIN: My house is clean. Is impossible. Meskolic a vee estroka. You eyes make tricking.

ISHMAEL: Yes. But I saw a mouse. I smelled it. It's a stinky mouse.

COFFIN: No stinky mouse.

ISHMAEL: I was hoping you could call an exterminator.

COFFIN: Never mouse. You have been bringing filth. If mouse you not have been cleaning. It come for filth. I keep clean.

ISHMAEL: My apartment is pristine, I just have a mouse. Please, will you call an exterminator?

COFFIN: No mouse.

ISHMAEL: But there is.

COFFIN: You pay me last month rent? No. You not paying me, but you want for me is paying exterminator? You have no mouse.

ISHMAEL: I started a new job today. I can pay you in full in two weeks. Last month and this month. And next month in advance.

COFFIN: You good tenant. And quiet. I hate to lose you. Even if you destiny is black-starred.

ISHMAEL: Excuse me?

COFFIN: A bad moon shines on you. Bad things come. Much bad things. I see in my tea this morning. Good night.

ISHMAEL: So, I'll just buy some traps then?

But she is gone.

Scene IV

A café. MRS STUBB is waiting. RACHEL enters hurriedly.

RACHEL: Hi Mom. Sorry I'm late. I got stuck on a streetcar.

MRS STUBB: Oh, don't worry about it dear.

RACHEL: The streetcar got jammed on the track and couldn't turn.

MRS STUBB: It's all right dear. You're an Artiste.

RACHEL: Mom.

MRS STUBB: What?

RACHEL: Nanty.

MRS STUBB: I said it's all right. *(Sighs.)* And in the real world we say "nothing", dear.

RACHEL: I just don't want to get off on the wrong foot, that's all.

MRS STUBB: Oh. I see. I'm supposed to apologize because you're late. Is that it?

RACHEL: No. It's my fault. I'm sorry. I should be more attentive to time. Especially when you're only in town for the afternoon.

MRS STUBB: I guess you just take after your father. He couldn't be any where on time either. and I don't suppose you keep a tight schedule in the circus—

RACHEL: We do actually—

MRS STUBB: Thank God you've given that up. I used to dream you'd been eaten by lions. I'd wake up all sweaty and screaming. It was awful!

RACHEL: Well, I've gone off.

MRS STUBB: The terror you put me through. Maybe the high wire would snap. Or you'd be taken advantage of by some sideshow freak! Some human torso with no arms or legs slithering into your cot or bunk and waiting in ambush, just lying there, pretending to be a pillow!

RACHEL: They're not freaks. They're called Human Oddities.

MRS STUBB: I'm just glad you've settled down.

RACHEL: I'm glad you're glad.

MRS STUBB: It's a start.

Silence.

RACHEL: Have you called any dukey?

MRS STUBB: Don't talk like that in front of me, Rachel. It's vulgar.

RACHEL: I don't mean to. It's habit. Have you ordered?

MRS STUBB: No. A boy keeps coming by and I keep sending him away. I don't think I'll have time for anything but coffee now.

RACHEL: Sorry.

MRS STUBB: A coffee with my only daughter is better than nothing. It beats a kick in the head.

RACHEL: The streetcar was finked.

MRS STUBB: I know dear. You told me.

WAITER enters.

WAITER: Are you ready to order yet?

MRS STUBB: Dear?

RACHEL: We'll just have two coffees.

MRS STUBB: Actually, I'll have a glass of your house red. If it's not too dry. And the bruschetta. *(She says bruskeeta).*

WAITER: Coming right up.

Pause.

MRS STUBB: Well, there's no sense in running off with an empty stomach. I might faint.

RACHEL: It's okay, Mom. I don't want to have a clem.

MRS STUBB: Are you dating anyone at the moment, honey? At least anyone you'll tell me about?

RACHEL: No. I'm not dating anyone. I'd tell you.

MRS STUBB: Dear. That's too bad. You're no spring chicken any more. Still, I guess it's better to be an old maid than to take up with the rats you used to drag home.

RACHEL: Hey, you'll never guess who joined our work!

MRS STUBB: Who, dear?

RACHEL: Do you remember Ishmael? He was a friend in high school.

MRS STUBB: Not a friend from high school! Is he on parole? Don't you dare get mixed up with that crowd again Rachel. Your job is an embarrassment, but you're too old to louse it up with self destructive hurly burly!

RACHEL: No, Ishmael wasn't part of that crowd. He was the mousy one you made me study with. With the bad hair. He's cuter now. He's grown into his face. He's still not my type.

MRS STUBB: Mm. Oh, that timid clever boy? That's a start.

RACHEL: It's not the start of anything.

MRS STUBB: What does he do at your office? Is he of the upwardly mobile class?

RACHEL: He has the same job as me.

MRS STUBB: The same job as you? Oh, darling. That's awful! What has he been doing with his life? Riding the rails, waiting for his face to grow? What a waste.

RACHEL: Mom, you don't even know him.

MRS STUBB: It's one thing for you to hold that job. You're a late starter, thanks to that damned sideshow phase. What's his excuse?

RACHEL: He's a fine jack!

MRS STUBB: Promise me you won't get mixed up with him. When I got that job for you, it was so you could get some stability, work your way up. I hoped my daughter would have the chance to drop her glass slipper in the foyers of a different class of men.

RACHEL: Mother—

MRS STUBB: I did not intend for you to forsake the potential Prince Charmings I lay at your feet in order to stagnate with the office rats and mice.

WAITER enters.

WAITER: One coffee. A glass of the house red. And the bruschetta.

He pronounces it bruschetta.

MRS STUBB: On second thought, I don't really have time to eat. Can you take this back?

RACHEL: Never mind. I'll eat it. *(WAITER looks confused.)* It's all right. She just being bull joey.

WAITER: Of course. Madame. Joey.

WAITER exits.

MRS STUBB: There's no need to make a scene in front of the waiter. I only wish you'd find a good, hard-working man who can take care of you before it's too late. Some one respectable who can provide for you and my future grandchildren, God willing.

RACHEL: Like Dad did?

MRS STUBB: That was uncalled for. You're getting old, you know.

RACHEL: Jiminy Christ. First, I'm not dating Ishmael. He's strictly Larry Koday.

MRS STUBB: He's who?

RACHEL: I don't want to date him. Secondly, if your whole whip and chair treatment to bully me into this lousy job was so I'll meet a pedagree stud and catch a litter before my clock winds down, you've got another think coming.

MRS STUBB: Rachel Stubb!

RACHEL: Thirdly… I guess there isn't a thirdly.

MRS STUBB: Honey, you know I'm only looking out for what's best for you.

RACHEL: No. There is a thirdly. I don't need you to look out for what's best for me. Maybe I used to. Maybe I was trouble to myself for a long time. But it's different now. I don't need anyone to look out for me but me. And if I want to date someone, I'll do it with or without your approval.

MRS STUBB: Don't you dare.

Silence.

Are you going to eat the bruskeeta darling, or can your poor mother have a bite?

Scene V

ISHMAEL's apartment. RACHEL can be seen off in the shadows, in some nether world, half lit.

ISHMAEL: I really want to ask Rachel out.[8] I always have. In high school, I was just too chicken. She knew how I felt, I think. and she might have even said yes, out of pity. But in a few weeks, she would have dumped me and I would have drowned my own remains in a deluge of pubescent tears. She hung out with a different crowd than I did. She actually

[8] This story is totally true, except the movie was *Pee Wee's Big Adventure*.

had a crowd with which to hang out. I just shared a cafeteria table with three guys with whom no one else would share a cafeteria table. However, after twelve years of dreaming about her, and then finally seeing her again, I had almost mustered up enough moxie to ask her to a movie, even though I was pretty certain she'd brush me off. But one thing held me back. That Mouse. But not just the Mouse—although that was almost enough—It was what the Mouse represented to me.

When I was thirteen years old, there was this girl in my class named Andrea Pispadekis. She didn't like anyone to call her that. She liked to be called Aundraya. So she would seem more exotic. She had beautiful dark eyes, and inviting, full lips. and I really liked her. I knew she liked me, because her best friend, Sabrina Newmeyer was dating my best friend, Brig Bodrug, and Brig said that Sabrina said that Aundraya liked me and I should ask her out. It was a plausible scenario. Aundraya touched my arm a lot when she talked to me. And she laughed at almost everything I said, even when it wasn't funny. She also had this peculiar habit of repeatedly brushing her hair behind her right ear, I think to show me her bare neck. So, I figured I had a pretty good shot. But I was terrified. What if—God forbid—I asked her out and she said no! Or worse, what if she said yes, and when it came time to kiss her, I didn't do it well enough and she dumped me, or laughed at me. Weeks went by, while I brooded and my sense of panic increased. Brig was mad at me. Brig said Sabrina was mad at me. Why was I wasting so much time?

Finally, one Sunday morning, I could stand the tension no more. I vowed that I would not waste another day. I phoned her, from my parents' bedroom, the most private phone in the house. Her father answered.

"Is Aundraya there?" I said. My voice cracked a little, and I think I heard him snicker.

RACHEL: *(As the DAD's voice.)* "Who?"

ISHMAEL: "Andrea. Is Andrea there."

RACHEL: *(As the DAD's voice.)* "Yes. She is."

ISHMAEL: "Can I speak to her?"

RACHEL: *(As the DAD's voice.)* "Yes, I imagine you can."

Pause.

ISHMAEL: "May I speak to her?" and then her funny, funny father went to get her. She picked up the phone and said...

RACHEL: *(Playing AUNDRAYA as a person, not a puppet.)* "Hello?"

ISHMAEL: And she sounded really nervous. Her respiration was shallow. I suppose I should have taken solace in the fact that she was as nervous as I, but the thought didn't occur to me at the time.

"I was going to go see a matinee of the *Breakfast Club* today, and I wondered if maybe you would like to go downtown to the movie theatre to see the matinee of the *Breakfast Club* with me to the matinee of the *Breakfast Club*."

She didn't say anything at first. But I could hear her making quiet hiccoughing noises.

RACHEL: *(As AUNDRAYA.)* "hic...hic...hic..."

ISHMAEL: Then she said...

RACHEL: *(As AUNDRAYA.)* "I can't today. I have to clean my hamster's cage."

ISHMAEL: Thus, leaving me with a bewildered queasy

sensation. I said a polite, shell-shocked goodbye and hung up.

If she'd said that she liked another boy, I would have been okay.

And I would have survived if she'd said I was just ugly. I had bad hair then.

Even if she told me to drop dead and never speak to her again, I would have pulled through.

But playing second fiddle to a hamster. I was being thrown over for a sullied rodent and his excrement. That's when I decided to run away and become a deep sea fisherman.

Aundraya and I never spoke again. Not even to say hello in the halls.

Within two weeks she was going with Marty Pomeranski and the two of them started double dating with Sabrina and Brig.

Eighteen years later, that wound was still festering. and no matter how courageous I tried to be, I was afraid to ask out Rachel, because that horrible white invader in my apartment made Aundraya's dung-caked hamster seem all too close. Besides, why would a beautiful circus star waste her time with on a file clerk who's afraid of a mouse?

Scene VI

ISHMAEL and RACHEL are in their office, performing a menial, mind-numbingly dull task.

ISHMAEL: Um, Rachel?

RACHEL: Yeah?

ISHMAEL: Never mind.

RACHEL: Okey.

Silence.

What did you do before you got your job in here in Hell? Rode the rails, trying to find yourself?

ISHMAEL: No. There was no rail-riding. I just submerged myself in university until they stopped awarding scholarships for prolonging adolescence. Is this an M513? Or a Graduated Payments Received?

RACHEL: That's a R77 slash A. It goes with the MIs. I wish I'd gone to university. Sometimes I feel like I'm good for planges in a Dog and Pony Show, but in the Towner world I'm strictly First of May.

ISHMAEL: The circus must provide a solid background in pragmatic anthropology.

RACHEL: I'm sure it does, but they don't hand out dictionaries with your unitard and greasepaint.

ISHMAEL: Uh, It must teach you a lot about human nature.

RACHEL: Like, "If you're not on the show you're a gilly. And if you're a gilly you're a rube"?

ISHMAEL: Sure.

RACHEL: Or fade on the slanger pen when you're ragging.

ISHMAEL: I have no idea what you just said.

RACHEL: Fun, eh? It means don't go near the lion cage when you're menstruating.

ISHMAEL: Why?

RACHEL: You smell like food.

ISHMAEL: See. I learned something already. Lions eat menstrual fluid. I bet most people go through their whole lives without knowing that.

RACHEL: Didn't they teach you anything in Unversity?

ISHMAEL: No. I received BA. In English. And a Masters. And a doctorate. And I didn't learn a darn thing. However, I read some exemplary books. Like *Moby Dick.* I wrote my thesis on it. "The White Whale as Phallus."

RACHEL: You're grifting.

ISHMAEL: Nope.

RACHEL: The teacher didn't laugh when you said, "My thesis is on *Moby Dick*[9] and you can call me Ishmael?"

ISHMAEL: Yes, my um...my professor did find it a jocular coincidence. Nonetheless, it was a meritorious paper. If I say so myself.

RACHEL: Shoot.

ISHMAEL: Ahab's peg leg is a symbol of erectile dysfunction and his pursuit of Moby Dick—obvious symbolism there: is an attempt to regain his potency. That's why there's so much text about the whale's spout. There's an entire chapter on spouting—it's a naked Freudian ejaculate metaphor. There are repeated allusions to Ahab's "sundered mast", meaning: textually: his peg leg. Subtextually, of course, it's his...uh...thingy. Furthermore there's a reference to Ahab on only leaving one dent in his marriage pillow, and when he married his young wife, he made her a widow. So forth.

RACHEL: So, it's an eight hundred page book about a guy who fishes because he can't get it up? That's useful dinkus.

ISHMAEL: Not really. What do I do with this?

[9] Just so you know, *Moby Dick* is my favourite book. I try to read it once a year. Every other year I skip the boring bits.

RACHEL: Is it stamped received?

ISHMAEL: Uh, no.

RACHEL: Lose it. You never saw it.

ISHMAEL: Okay.

RACHEL: What else?

ISHMAEL: I telemarketed for a while selling duct cleaning. As soon as you say "duct cleaning", four out of five people—excluding the ones who hang up—quack at you. One day I spent an entire shift—five straight hours—phoning my answering machine so I wouldn't have to hear any more duck sounds. I figured then it was time to quit.[10] I worked in a Latin bookstore until it went under. Then I hid in my apartment and ate Cheetos for a few months. And now I work here. It's not as thrilling as life in the circus, is it? I should have gone to sea like we said.

RACHEL: That's okay. Being on the show wasn't all St Louis on Aba-dabba. You don't really get to meet any one other than troupers... You missed this F23. Bildad will kill you... Things get pretty incestuous pretty quickly. Sooner or later you've slept with just about everybody.

ISHMAEL: Oh.

RACHEL: University's probably like that too. Lots of cot hopping.

ISHMAEL: Well, there were cots. I never really mastered the hopping.

RACHEL: Oh.

ISHMAEL: Did you...um...anyone serious.

[10] I really did this. For months, actually. Eventually my answering machine broke, and then I quit.

RACHEL: We shouldn't really get into it while we're working. It's a long act.

ISHMAEL: I'll file and listen. Look. My fingers and ears work independently of one another. I'm braced for your rogues' gallery of exotic lovers and foreign princes.

RACHEL: Okay. First, I never made it with a foreign prince. A few pitchmen, God help me. A ponger or two.

ISHMAEL: A what?

RACHEL: A ponger. An acrobat. I dated two of them. Three, technically. One was conjoined twins. And a lion tamer for a while, Tashtego, Lord of the Beasts. Boy oh boy, he was something, but something else too, you know. A pitchman, he was a louse but I wanted some help with my public speaking. Two joeys—clowns, that is—I dated them concurrently. One was good for laughs but nothing serious. The other was serious but about as uplifting as elephant flop. Oh, and I dated an elephant trainer. I forget his name. And the Great Dagoo. Sort of. He was the catcher in my swing act. We fooled around now and then, but I never let him go all the way. It was a safety issue. I figured a catcher is less likely to drop you if he thinks he might get lucky. After he's been there, he's likely to get sloppy. And a bunch of other flatties, all rats. Finally wound up with a Lithuanian picture gallery, and after that there was nowhere to go but off.

ISHMAEL: Picture gallery?

RACHEL: A tattooed man. He was a rat too. Six months with him. Yuck. And then I just got sick of kicking sawdust. I thought, I'm almost thirty, my clock is like tick-tickety-boom. I need some security. So I went off the show, split with the gallery. And now I earn my alfalfa here. My mother's idea. If your mother's not making you work here, you should quit. But first, file these in with the prescanned catalogue amendments. Tashtego was the worst— the lion tamer. He'd slept with anything with legs the whole time we were shacking together. Everyone knew it. Even me. He didn't even try to hide it. I just couldn't bring myself to split with him.

ISHMAEL: How come?

RACHEL: Well, he was gorgeous. Muscular and hot. He had this great European accent. It was bunkus, he was from a farm in Moose Jaw. But it was a tempting toot-up. He never said nanty, just growled a lot. So when he said even a word or two, it like: *(She makes a lustful noise.)*. That's what I found so hard to slip— If he wanted something he grabbed it in his big, rough mittens. That's what made him such a bastard in the first place.

ISHMAEL: A preponderance of id over superego?

RACHEL: No, he was egotistical all right. But I'm hook and line for a jack with a good brasserie. If he burst in here right now, and said, "Roar!", I don't know if I'd say Nix. I'm a rube for jacks like that.

Pause.

ISHMAEL: Are you busy this weekend?

RACHEL: What?

ISHMAEL: I'm free. I was wondering if you were free.

BILDAD enters.

BILDAD: Mr— Uh and Miss Stubbs! I have just come from Mr Peleg's office where he chided me for a slow-down of productivity in this, my department. I assured him that my employees, you, were working both diligently, and to the best of your ability. "Sir," I said. "My department is ship-shape." And what do I find upon leaving his office!

I find two workers in my employ gabber-jawing when they should be backlog clearing.

RACHEL: Sorry, Mr Bildad.

ISHMAEL: It was my fault, Mr Bildad.

BILDAD: See that it doesn't happen again Mr...um...Mister!

He exits. RACHEL and ISHMAEL whisper.

RACHEL: Shriveled up little quarter pole.

ISHMAEL: Who's Mr Peleg?

RACHEL: He's the Boss Canvas Man. The president. His Phineas T is on your nut.

ISHMAEL: I haven't met him yet. Is he as charming as his toady?

RACHEL: He's as charming as bull flap.

They work silently.

RACHEL: You were asking me something?

ISHMAEL: Oh. No. Yes. Hm. It wasn't really of crucial import. Did you notice where I put the R77s? I'd hate to incur our masters' wrath.

RACHEL: I am free this weekend.

ISHMAEL: You are?

RACHEL: Yes. Are you asking me out?

ISHMAEL: Well, yes. I suppose I am.

RACHEL: On a date? Or as an old friend?

ISHMAEL: I hadn't really. As a date, I guess.

RACHEL: Really?

ISHMAEL: Yes. If that's too weird, it's fine. We don't have to. I know I'm not a big brutish lion kinker. Maybe we could just, you know...

RACHEL: Sure, I'll go out on a date with you.

ISHMAEL: You would?

RACHEL: Let's just not get our hopes up though. It would be a muck run if we went into this pie-eyed and finked it up. What did you have in mind?

ISHMAEL: Um.

RACHEL: Why don't I just come over to your pad room and we can have a tipple, and see what to do from there.

ISHMAEL: My place? Sure. Uh...No. Um, I could meet you at your place.

RACHEL: I have roommates. They're awfully nosey. It would be hard for us to find privacy.

ISHMAEL: Privacy?

RACHEL: Yeah. I find dates go better without spectators.

ISHMAEL: My place isn't...the best place. I'm having problems with a mou—a mess. My place is infested with mess... Let's have a picnic! Down by the beach. I'll throw some libations together and we can meander along the board walk. Maybe sit on the escarpment and ponder the water. How's that sound?

RACHEL: Okay. That sounds good.

ISHMAEL: Good.

Scene VII

ISHMAEL plops down on his couch, dropping his hat on a cushion. He picks up his book and begins to read. Slowly his hat starts to crawl away, as if pulled along by some hideous creature underneath it. ISHMAEL notices something is amiss, and turns to face the moving hat. Too late. It has jumped behind the couch, unseen. ISHMAEL shrugs and returns to his book. GRENDELMAUS leaps up from behind the couch and pounces on ISHMAEL's head. ISHMAEL screams. Blackout.

Scene VIII

ISHMAEL and RACHEL are having a picnic by the lake.

ISHMAEL: I had a girlfriend in first year, Eliza Po, who taught me that there are only three kinds of noses in the whole world, and that every human being, of any race, creed or colour, can be classified by these three nose types: Nasus libumi. The Bun, which is flatish, with wider, rounded nostrils. Eliza had a cute bun. But a nasty temper. I considered doing my post-doc on that, the Relationship Between Nose Shapes and Temperament. Sort of a twentieth century update on the theory of medieval humours.

Pause while RACHEL doesn't laugh. A flying insect appears and begins circling ISHMAEL's head.

There is Nasus Piscis, the fish, of which I am a classic example.

RACHEL: What makes you a fish?

ISHMAEL: You see how it slopes inward in a smooth arc and then swoops back out like a ski jump?

RACHEL: Uh-huh.

ISHMAEL: Fish.

RACHEL: What kind of temperament does that make you?

ISHMAEL: I couldn't find a correlation. That's why I don't have a post-doc. Shoo!

The bug departs.

RACHEL: What's my nose?

ISHMAEL: You're nose is of the third variety, Nasus Equus. You're a horse.

RACHEL: I beg your pardon?

ISHMAEL: A horse. See it goes out, then there's a little bump, and then it slides down. It's a Horse. There's nothing wrong with that.

RACHEL: Uh-huh. I know one flatty who's not getting a kiss at the end of this date.

ISHMAEL: You were going to kiss me?

RACHEL: I was thinking about letting you kiss me. But now nanty. Your lips might stick in my bridle.

ISHMAEL: It's not a bad horse. It's a pretty little horse. A very pretty, little, Shetland pony horse.

The bug returns.

RACHEL: Like the high school's Little People ride in dressage.

ISHMAEL: What?

RACHEL: Circus joke. Like your hysterical medieval humour gag.

ISHMAEL: Look, horse noses are my favourite. Don't be upset. Scat!

The bug exits.

RACHEL: I'm not upset. I'm just hungry. Is there any more hay?

ISHMAEL: I think it's in the basket beside the worms.

RACHEL: Worms?

ISHMAEL: For my fish.

RACHEL: Is that why we're eating here, by the lake? So your beezer will be close to home?

The bug returns.

ISHMAEL: "Take any path you please, and ten to one it carries you to water." Herman Melville.

RACHEL: "Show me a guy who believes in magic, and I'll show you a guy who's paid two bits to see a horse with a gaffed up horn." P.T. Barnum.[11]

The bug lands in whatever ISHMAEL is eating, just as he takes a bite.

ISHMAEL: Ew! Bug! Bleh!

RACHEL: In your food? That's really, really bad luck.

ISHMAEL: It is?

RACHEL: Bug in your duke, your cheat wire's fluked.

ISHMAEL: Sorry?

RACHEL: It's a circus saying.

ISHMAEL: It had that ring to it.

RACHEL: Turn around and spit in each direction.

ISHMAEL: Come on.

RACHEL: I'm serious.

ISHMAEL: Well, a fluke, that's a good thing right?

RACHEL: No, fluked, it means frayed. Your safety wire is frayed and you'll crash and die. It's a bad thing.

[11] Actually, I made this up. Barnum never said anything of the kind.

ISHMAEL: I don't have a safety wire.

RACHEL: It's a whaddayacallit. Turn and spit.

He does.

ISHMAEL: Am I safe now?

RACHEL: Probably not. Now you're supposed to rub a chimp head.

ISHMAEL: I don't have one of those.

RACHEL: Show folk see bad omens in everything. You're screwed no matter what you do.

ISHMAEL: Well, now that my days are numbered, I should make my confession.

RACHEL: Okay.

ISHMAEL: I used to have the biggest crush on you. In high school. I thought you were...you know.

RACHEL: That's a confession? I'm glad we didn't go out then. I would have chewed you up for tanbark.

ISHMAEL: I'm just not adventurous, I guess.

RACHEL: No. I needed to tickle the wild calliope till it was out of my system. If we'd gone out then, it would have finked up all sour and ugly, and we wouldn't be having this lovely picnic now.

ISHMAEL: I think you're beautiful.

RACHEL: Even with my horse.

ISHMAEL: Yeah. A shame about that.

RACHEL: Why?

ISHMAEL: Because I'd try to kiss you now, if I hadn't offended you.

RACHEL: Maybe if you sneak up on me, you'll get to my lips before I spot you.

ISHMAEL: You think?

RACHEL: You can't win if you don't play, Rube.

They kiss.

Damn. You snuck up on me.

Scene IX[12]

RACHEL sits on a stool beside the Punch and Judy stage.

RACHEL: Spurred by diabolical malice and hatred for the human race, Grendelmaus roamed the wide Earth, searching for foul deeds to perform.

EDDY enters.

EDDY: It's such a beautiful day. I think I'll donate all my money to the orphanage.

GRENDELMAUS enters.

Oh. Hello there, little mousy.

GRENDELMAUS bites off his head.

RACHEL: But solitude takes its toll, even on the most devilish of blackened souls, and as the centuries wore on, Grendelmaus found himself yearning for companionship. He longed to find a love to comfort him through the endless passage of time.

A HOOKER enters.

HOOKER: Love for sale. Appetizing young love for sale.

[12] This next bit is pretty much stolen from the gothic romance *Melmoth the Wander*. In the tradition of Gothic Romances, I've stolen it without naming it as a source.

GRENDELMAUS approaches her and they copulate.

(Without much interest.) Ya, baby. Don't stop. O Ya. That'll be seventeen samolians.

He bites off her head and exits.

RACHEL: Meanwhile, in the uncharted oceans at the edge of the world, a merchant ship sailed upon the waves. The skies grew dim, and lightning sundered the mainmast and the ship was swallowed by the sea. All aboard were drowned, save for one solitary baby who was ferried to a deserted tropical island on the glistening back of a friendly trout.

We see this happen.

The girl grew up alone on the island, without ever knowing human companionship. Her sole companions were the birds, and the trees and the lizards of the forest. They fed her and kept her clothed and warm and taught her to speak in their strange tongues. The girl was happy but lonely. And since she never learned the perfidious ways of humankind, her heart alone on earth remained pure and unsullied. Far off, on the mainland, Grendelmaus heard tell of this beautiful, untainted girl. The evil mouse vowed to find her and destroy her goodness. It would be his greatest triumph, to ruin a maiden as virtuous as he was vile.

GRENDELMAUS laughs diabolically. Exits. We see the GIRL alone on her island. Birds flit happily around her, twittering. She twitters back and they have a nice little chat. GRENDELMAUS enters ominously.

GIRL: Hello there. Who are you? I haven't seen a creature like you before. Would you like to play with me? We can drop flower petals into the water and watch them float like little boats.

GRENDELMAUS: Huzzah! You're beautiful.

GIRL: What's that?

GRENDELMAUS: Can I stay here and sit with you? I'd like to be your friend.

GIRL: Okay. I've never had a friend before.

RACHEL: Much to Grendelmaus's surprise, he fell in love with the charming innocent, and suddenly harming her was the furthest thing from his mind. In time, wooed by his kindness and companionship, the girl found that she had fallen in love with him. When Grendelmaus realized this, it tore his heart in two.

GRENDELMAUS: I must leave you. Today.

GIRL: But why! I love you! My soul belongs with yours! I want to become a part of you!

GRENDELMAUS: You don't know what that means. I am evil, fully to the bottom of my blackened soul. Cain's mark is on my brow. Nothing but monstrosity lurks inside me. If I stay with you now, you'll become tarnished through your love for me, and I cannot bear to see your innocence destroyed. I must leave. Forever.

GIRL: Stay! I love you.

GRENDELMAUS: I go because I love you.

RACHEL: And Grendelmaus left the island, never to return. In time a ship came and the girl was rescued. She grew older, and her love faded. One day she met and fell in love with a wealthy young man from the city, a man named Stubb whose nose was of the Horse Variety. She married him, and they had children with horse noses, and their children had children with horse noses, and so the name of Stubb, and the Stubb Family Nasus Equus was passed on from generation to generation.

Scene X

ISHMAEL's apartment. ISHMAEL and the Mouse are locked in a fearsome stare. ISHMAEL reaches under a cushion and pulls out a hammer. The MOUSE reaches behind a cushion and pulls out an extremely lethal-looking meat cleaver. They skirmish madly.

Scene XI

ISHMAEL enters hardware store. Looks around the shelves. Can't seem to find what he wants. Enter a CLERK.[13]

CLERK: Help y'find sompthin?

ISHMAEL: Yeah. I...uh...I have this really smart mouse. Like Immanuel Kant smart.

CLERK: Y'tried the traditional wooden spring trap?

ISHMAEL: Yeah. It caught nanty.

CLERK: You tried the little glue dishes? They step in em and their foot gets stuck so they try t'chew themselves out. Then their mouth and nose fills up with glue and their heart and lungs explode. Bango!

ISHMAEL: No good.

CLERK: We got glue paper. It's what they use in the good restaurants. I've seen 'em catch four or five mice a night. Smell it! See that? Smell's like cheese 'n bacon flavour. Same as they use in potato chips.

ISHMAEL: He saw right through it.

CLERK: Maybe you should buy a cat.

[13] Again, the following is autobiographical. Except for the bit with the Old One-legged Man.

ISHMAEL: I break out in hives.

CLERK: Might as well sign over your lease to the mouse then. Sometimes the mice win.

ISHMAEL: You've got to have something.

CLERK: Sorry, buddy.

ISHMAEL: I just can't stand the feeling of being invaded. I think about it all the time. I'm always looking over my shoulder to see if it's there. I can't relax. I'm wound up like a ukulele string.

CLERK: I don't have anything else to help you.

ISHMAEL: I've started to see this woman, see? She's fantastic. I've had a thing for her since I was a kid. My first wet dream was about her, for Chrissake. All my life I've dreamed about making love to her. The touch of her skin. I bet it's so soft. And the curve of her belly. And I've imagined each little hidden freckle. You understand? And I think things are headed that way. Now I feel like I had a shot, a one-in-a-million one-time chance of being happy with the girl of my dreams. And I know, I just know, if I bring her home, and that damn mouse is prowling around, I won't...I'll be too worried about it jumping out. Or running across the backs of our naked legs. Or hopping up on the pillow and making a nest in her hair. Or leaping between us and hissing at me just as we're about to...couple. I'm afraid I won't be able to...relax about it, you know. For Chrissake, she used to sleep with a guy who punched out lions for a living, and I'm scared erectionless by one little white rodent.

CLERK: Sorry, pal. I work in a hardware store. I'm not like a sex psychiatrist er nuthin.

The CLERK exits. A dwarfish, peg-legged OLD MAN pops out.

OLD MAN: Did ye say ye wast having foul truck with a mouse?

ISHMAEL: Yeah.

OLD MAN: Ist it a white mouse? With a knotted brow, like the mark of Cain? And a long, hairless tail wound up like a cork-screw?

ISHMAEL: Yes!

OLD MAN: Dost it have a fiery glint in its eye, like hot coals from the Devil's Bouge? And does its cursed proboscis crook slightly to the starboard side as if to stand askance of it's own rank, effluvient stench?

ISHMAEL: Yes. That's it! That's my Mouse!

OLD MAN: It ist the Grendelmaus ye hast seen, lad. And a fouler demon didst never spring from the fiery pit! Ye art cursed to have its damned paws patter cross thy wake!

ISHMAEL: You know it then?

OLD MAN: Know it? Ay! I know it. It fell upon me when I wast but a boy. Tore off me leg as I slept and beat me with it. Imagine the terror of a sweet virgin boy to wake in mortal pain and see a musculine hobgoblin wailing upon his boyish brow with the bloody stump of his own freshly sundered limb! Ay, I know the Grendelmaus. *(He spits.)* Yaweh's wrath upon it!

ISHMAEL: What can I do. How can I catch it?

OLD MAN: No trap built by mortal man canst catch it, me lad. Grendelmaus ist old as the Earth, and elder brother to man. It hast walked the path of Nod, with his mother, Lillith. And seen the dark days when the Great Old Ones ruled the world. Ye needs magic to stop it, boy.

ISHMAEL: Magic.

OLD MAN: I hast in my possession of book of such primeval arcana as could rid ye of him. I'll sell it to ye, for a price.

ISHMAEL: Name it.

OLD MAN: Bring me the demon's right hindmost limb when ye hast slain it, that I might hang it upon my wooden one which serves to mark the mast it purloined from me all those years ago...

ISHMAEL: It's a deal.

OLD MAN: Then here, lad. *(The OLD MAN hands ISHMAEL an old dusty tome.)*

ISHMAEL: What's this? A rat catcher's manual?

OLD MAN: Har. The book holds power for many things. The power to make dry the rolling oceans, or raise a forest from a house plant. But it'll serve thy needs with the mouse. In this tome ist writ a rite, which shall summon for you the aid of a familiar spirit, like the djinn of old. Many tasks canst it perform for ye, but waste it not. The Grendelmaus is cunning and can sniff out necromancy. And it may have magic of its own. Vanquish it swiftly lest it seize the initiative and cause the tide to turn and pull ye under the foamy brine!

ISHMAEL: I will.

OLD MAN: When all ist done, bring back the book and limb to me and we shall consider thy debts fulfilled.

ISHMAEL: Thanks. I'll do that.

OLD MAN: Remember, Grendelmaus is cunning. Strike ye foremost and without warning.

ISHMAEL: Yeah. You bet.

OLD MAN: Heed me, Boy! Strike first or ye be lost!

Exeunt severally.

Scene XII

ISHMAEL enters with a bag full of strange things, and the book. He puts a large crock pot on the floor and plugs it in.

ISHMAEL: *(Reading.)* Simmer, Simmer; Dark grow dimmer!

He pulls the ingredients from the bag and drops them, as they are named into the crock pot.

Hair of mongrel, wing of bird,
Bovine gizzard, monkey's turd,
Claw of chicken, pig's foot too,
Tablespoon of wart of ewe.

There is no wart of ewe in the bag.

Great. Where am I going to find wart of ewe at this time of night?

He looks in his fridge, finds a package of hot dogs, rips off a bit of one and drops it in the pot.

Tablespoon of wart of ewe.
Stoke the cauldron, flames burn brightly!
Sautee briefly, simmer lightly!
Simmer, Simmer: Dark grow dimmer!
Blood of virgin, bachelor's nail

He uses his own.

Eye of mackerel, ginger ale.
Ginger ale and virgin blood? This is ridiculous.
To culminate this potent brew, Speak incantation, whisk it through:
I'R'lyeh Cthu—

There is a knock at the door.

Just a minute!

He moves the crock pot into another room. and answers the door. It's RACHEL.

RACHEL: Hi there, sailor.

ISHMAEL: Hi.

RACHEL: Surprised?

ISHMAEL: Uh, yeah. A little. How did you know where I live?

RACHEL: Phone book. Didn't take a college degree. I was in the neighbourhood, and I had this bottle of wine, and a rented movie, and I thought you might want to have a tipple and watch it with me.

ISHMAEL: What's the film?

RACHEL: I don't know. Can I come in?

ISHMAEL: Sure. Please. Yeah. I'll take your coat.

He does. She is dressed invitingly.

RACHEL: Glasses in the kitchen?

ISHMAEL: Yes. I'll get some. Um. Two of them. For us.

Fetches two wine glasses from the kitchen. He sniffs inquisitively. She seats herself on the couch. He returns and begins fumbling with the bottle.

RACHEL: You have a nice home sweet home. It's cozy, like you.

ISHMAEL: It's sufficient. There are some…uh…inadequacies.

He opens the bottle and pours. She pats the couch beside her. He sits. She raises her glass.

RACHEL: To pals reunited.

ISHMAEL: Mm-hm.

They drink.

RACHEL: I didn't really bring a movie.

ISHMAEL: No?

RACHEL: I was sitting in my pad room thinking about you. We've been going around for three weeks, and you've only kissed me.

ISHMAEL: Yes. Well. That's...while true...is...

RACHEL: Maybe it's me. Or maybe you're shy. You need some prompting to speed things along.

ISHMAEL: The latter is...but—

RACHEL: So, I invited myself over. To prompt you. I'm going to prompt you now.

ISHMAEL: You can prompt me. Prompting is good. It's good to be prompted.

RACHEL: There's just one thing. I'm pretty sure you're mooning for me.

ISHMAEL: I am. For sure.

RACHEL: Sh. I'm worried that what you're attracted to is like a mental snap-shot of what I used to be. I'm the jill that got away. The days when you were first of May and the whole world was things that could be, not things that weren't. Maybe life's disappointing to you and you want to catch your youth back. Maybe it's not really the real me you want at all. And maybe that's why you're so shy about moving things along. If you stay in front of the ring-bank it's all tinsel and big show and flash. When you get up close it's sweat and bull flap.

ISHMAEL: That's not it. I...I care about you...because...how do I say this— You're talking about Jungian anima projection, and why wouldn't you. It's... a...obvious concern given our relative...mine mostly...psychologies. But... *(Inhales.)* There's this verse in the Gnostic gospels, which is an ancient Coptic text circa three BC about man and woman being imperfect, just demi-beings, half-souls, incomplete on their own. And posessed of only fractured homunculi, we're vulnerable to evil influences that can invade us through the fissures left by our missing halves—like...evil rodents crawling in through an open wall. But when we fall in...when we embark on an amorous partnership, we find our other half and the fissure is closed. *(Pause.)* Maybe I'm not being clear.

RACHEL: I just never heard of this agnostic thing.

ISHMAEL: Sorry. I was a lousy lecturer.

RACHEL: No. This just isn't what I'm used to. There's usually less talking. *(Pause.)* I really like you. I don't want to get scared and take a jump.

ISHMAEL: I won't hurt you.

RACHEL: It was more the other way around.

ISHMAEL: Oh.

RACHEL: Make love to me.

ISHMAEL: Now? You mean now?

RACHEL: Was that too slutty?

ISHMAEL: No. No. I liked it.

They kiss.

ISHMAEL: Do you smell something?

RACHEL: No.

ISHMAEL: I thought I heard a smell.

RACHEL: Heard a smell?

ISHMAEL: Saw one, I mean. Forget it.

They kiss again. ISHMAEL breaks, sniffs.

RACHEL: What?

ISHMAEL: What what?

RACHEL: You seem distracted.

ISHMAEL: No. I...my nose was running. But it's better now. *(Sniffs.)* Yup, nothing there. All clear.

He kisses her.

ISHMAEL: You don't smell that?

RACHEL: *(Sniffs.)* No. *(She kisses him fully.)*

ISHMAEL: *(With his mouth full, so to speak.)* Okay then. No problem.

The MOUSE sneaks out and peers at ISHMAEL over RACHEL's shoulder. He starts. The MOUSE disappears.

RACHEL: What is it?

ISHMAEL: Nothing.

He resumes kissing her. She slides out of her dress, revealing elegant lingerie underneath. GRENDELMAUS appears and disappears again. ISHMAEL is breathless, and darts his eyes around the apartment. She unbuttons his shirt. As she's kissing his chest, moving towards his belt, which she is beginning to unfasten, he sits up.

RACHEL: What's wrong?

ISHMAEL: Nose again. Sorry. That's the thing. You meet a pretty girl and suddenly it's boogers all over the place.[14]

RACHEL: Is this too fast for you?

[14] Said by the great Rolland Sawatsky as an excuse for not talking to a girl who was giving him the eye in a bar in Germany. Fortunately, he overcame his reserve and necked with her mere moments later. Unfortunately, she turned out to be attending her own engagement party in the hotel bar. Rolland saw her the next morning engaged in a very dour discussion with a very distraught young German boy, who one can only assume to have been the former future groom.

ISHMAEL: I've dreamed about this since puberty. It's not too fast.

They resume. ISHMAEL is edgy and distracted.

RACHEL: Something's wrong.

ISHMAEL: Just a minute.

RACHEL: What?

ISHMAEL: I have to go to the kitchen...where...because I keep my...prophylactics there and...and I'd hate to interrupt things...once they were at an...less convenient place to interrupt them.

RACHEL: Okay. *(Aside.)* I feel *so* pretty.

ISHMAEL scampers off to the kitchen, plugs in the crock pot, and stirs it.

ISHMAEL: Simmer, simmer: Dark grow dimmer.
To culminate this potent brew,
Speak incantation, whisk it through:
I'R'lyeh Cthulhu f'tagen!

A large, winged DJINN blossoms forth from the crock pot. It is a terrifying reptilian apparition with tentacles hanging from its face.

DJINN: Ia! Ia! Cthulhu f'tagen! Ph'nglui mglw'nafh Cthulhu R'lyeh wgah-nagl f'tagen!

ISHMAEL: Shh!

DJINN: Who hast summoned me from my primordial slumber beneath the black abyss?

ISHMAEL: That would be me?

DJINN: Were it not that I am bound and enslaved by the ancient necromancy of Abdul Alhazred, I would sunder thee limb from limb and drag thy soul to my sulphurous layer in R'lyeh City, where I would feast upon thy ectoplasm for centuries to come. But bidst me serve thee, and I shall.

ISHMAEL: Um. How do I put this? I have a...a lady friend over. and I'm a little anxious. About this Mouse in the apartment and it's interfering with my...well my functionality, if you follow me.

DJINN: Speakest thou clearly, master and I shall execute thy bidding.

ISHMAEL: I'm entertaining a woman. and we'd like to get to know each other, in a knowing each other sort of sense, but I'm too distracted to consummate the: the knowing each other part.

DJINN: Limnst thou thy problem plainly and my power shall alieve thee.

ISHMAEL: I'm too freaked out by the mouse in my apartment to get it up.

DJINN: Then I shall raise up thy manhood like Babel's tower and enforce it with such stalwart potency that not even Yaweh's thunder should strike it down.

ISHMAEL: Fabulous. Please. Go.

The DJIN casts a spell. ISHMAEL is relieved of his burden. The DJIN disappears. RACHEL enters, holding some prophylactics.

RACHEL: If you can't find them, I happened to notice these in my purse.

ISHMAEL kisses her passionately and they tumble back to the bed.

Blackout.[15]

[15] Due to an unfortunate clause in our theatre rental agreement, we placed an intermission here. There is really no need for you to have one. Unless you're renting from the same theatre, in which case, here's a good place for one.

Scene XIII

RACHEL is at the puppet theatre.

RACHEL: Once upon a time, when mankind was but a glimmer in creations's eye, demented gods, known as the Great Old Ones ruled the Earth.[16]

A MONSTER 1 and MONSTER 2 enter.

MONSTER 1: We are the things that were and shall be again!

MONSTER 2: Dead by dawn!

MONSTER 1: Swallow your soul! Swallow your soul!

MONSTER 2: Dead by dawn![17]

The MONSTERS exit, muttering as their powers fade.

RACHEL: In time their powers faded and they were consigned to the shadows, lurking in the borders of the night, waiting to snare wary wanderers in their flaming maws.

A MAN, reading a book, wanders by. A MONSTER pounces out and eats him, and spits out the bloody, grisly parts.

MONSTER: Mmm. Pig flesh and mead.

RACHEL: The Grendelmaus was such a demon, matchless in evil, ruthless in his cunning.

GRENDELMAUS enters.

GRENDELMAUS: Morning, Carl.

MONSTER: How's tricks?

GRENDELMAUS: Tore the leg off a sailor boy while he slept this morning.

[16] All this is true. The Great Old Ones now lay sleeping in R'lyeh City and are dreaming of the day they will awake and claim the Earth once more. It's true.
[17] *Evil Dead 2.* Also a true story.

MONSTER: Still pining for your red-headed island girl?

GRENDELMAUS: Swallow your head, Carl.

GRENDELMAUS exits huffily.

MONSTER: Whipped little turd.

He exits too.

RACHEL: Long ago, in the desert of Skete, wandered a tortured nomad who sought to purge his fierce insanity in the flaming desert sand.

ALHAZRED enters. He tries to quell his madness, to no avail.

A window had opened in the lunatic's tormented brain, and he could see things other people couldn't. The dim monsters in the shadows blazed for him, in sharp relief.

The MONSTER is back.

MONSTER: I smell a fresh soul!

The MONSTER begins to torture ALHAZRED.

RACHEL: With his fevered, sun-scorched hand, he scribbled his untamed revelations into a book bound in human skin and inked in blood. He covered the pages with potent necromancy that would harness the demons, and bend them to human will.

ALHAZRED produces the Necronomicon and opens it.

ALHAZRED: I cadre sadre non-potis![18]

The MONSTER dies fantastically.

RACHEL: But being insane, the nomad also filled the book

[18] Boris Karloff's Satanic rite from *The Black Cat*. It's more or less Latin, and means, more or less, "To be taken with a grain of salt."

with incantations—that were they to fall into evil hands—could imbue the demons with powers beyond their twisted, diabolic dreams.

ALHAZRED exits with the book. GRENDELMAUS enters and stares after him.

RACHEL: And so the Great Old Ones both coveted and feared the book because, though it could destroy evil, it could also grant evil's most cherished wish.

Scene XIV

ISHMAEL and RACHEL are cozied up in bed, both smiling.

ISHMAEL: Psst. Rachel? Rachel, are you asleep?

RACHEL: Yes.

ISHMAEL: Me too.

Silence.

ISHMAEL: Rachel, I think I love you.

Silence.

RACHEL: *(Barely conscious.)* What?

ISHMAEL: I'm glad you're here. Goodnight.

RACHEL: Okay.

As ISHMAEL and RACHEL sleep. ISHMAEL sniffs furtively in his sleep. GRENDELMAUS enters, peels back the sheet, which covers RACHEL and admires her sleeping body. He smiles, kisses her on the cheek. She smiles in her sleep.

GRENDELMAUS looks about and finds the book near the bed. He takes it in his mouth and whacks ISHMAEL over the head with it. ISHMAEL and GRENDELMAUS stare at each other. ISHMAEL is terrified. He dives for the book, but GRENDELMAUS escapes without a trace.

RACHEL wakes up.

What's wrong?

ISHMAEL: Nothing. I thought I lost something that's all.

RACHEL: Can I help you find it?

ISHMAEL: No. It's okay. Everything's fine.

RACHEL: I had the strangest dream. I dreamed I was stranded on a desert island and a Mouse wanted to have my baby. I had sex with him for three thousand years and then he swam off, and you came by in a ship to rescue me, but when you heard about the Mouse, you sailed off to harpoon him, and you left me stuck there.

ISHMAEL: Really?... That's stupid. Why would you dream a stupid thing like that?

RACHEL: I don't know. I'm just stupid, I guess.

He waits till she appears to fall asleep, then sneaks from the bed, dresses furtively and exits.

ISHMAEL: Hardware store!

Scene XV

There is the sound of a large explosion. The hardware store CLERK is on stage, dazed and distraught. ISHMAEL enters hurriedly, still only half dressed. Sirens are heard in the distance. They grow louder as the scene progresses.

ISHMAEL: Hey, mister! You okay?

CLERK: Huh? How... What's this about?

ISHMAEL: Your hardware store. It's exploded. Are you okay?

CLERK: Did you smell it too?

ISHMAEL: Smell what?

CLERK: That smell in the pest control section. That awful smell. What's? Am I drunk?

ISHMAEL: The old man who works in your store, is he still inside?

CLERK: Ain't no one works here but me. I work alone.

ISHMAEL: Oh my God. I left her alone! Mister, I need you to pay attention. Someone might be in trouble! Where is the old man? I need his help.

CLERK: I don't know no old man. Did I say it was hot in here?

ISHMAEL: Listen! I left this woman alone with this Mouse and there's going to be trouble unless I can find the old man with the wooden leg to help me get his book back.

CLERK: Yer talking crazy talk. I was inside. Wasn't I inside?

ISHMAEL: Your store exploded. You were thrown through the window.

CLERK: I don' understan' ya. We're not open.

ISHMAEL: Don't move. The fire trucks are coming.

CLERK: Oh my God. I think my store exploded.

Scene XVI

ISHMAEL enters his apartment cauciously. He carries a rusty pipe or some such weapon. He looks about anxiously. No one is there.

ISHMAEL: *(Whispers.)* Rachel. Rachel, are you here?

He hears a scratching. He whirls to face it. Silence.

Rachel?

We hear sinister giggling from another direction. It fades away. ISHMAEL backs out of the apartment.

Scene XVII

ISHMAEL enters the office. He looks panicked and haggard. Soot streaks his face. RACHEL is not at her desk. He seems concerned about that. He begins to sit, stops suddenly then picks something carefully off the seat of his chair. It is a loaded mouse trap.

ISHMAEL: Mother of crap.

BILDAD enters.

BILDAD: You're late, this morning, Mr…uh. You're very late.

ISHMAEL: I'm very sorry, sir. I had an emergency of a personal nature this morning and it held me up.

BILDAD: It's unacceptable. It will make a very bad impression on Mr Fedallah.

ISHMAEL: On whom?

BILDAD: Oh my. No one has told you. Mr Peleg was found dead early this morning, the victim of a tragic freak accident.

ISHMAEL: An accident?

BILDAD: He fell face first into a bowl of glue, and clogged his mouth and nostrils. Poor man, his heart and lungs exploded. The board of directors despaired of finding a suitable replacement, but by a startling coincidence, Mr Fedallah's resume was submitted this morning, and his credentials were so astounding, they hired him on the spot. Mr Fedallah is our company's new president.

ISHMAEL: And you think that's a coincidence?

BILDAD: Perhaps, you're right, Mr… What *is* your name?

ISHMAEL: Ishmael, sir.

BILDAD: Ishman. Good. I'll be sure to tell Mr Fedallah. He said this morning that he wishes to know each employee by name. Such a charming man! What was I saying?

ISHMAEL: That Mr Peleg's death, and the sudden appearance of this mysterious Mr Fedallah is too unlikely to be a coincidence.

BILDAD: Yes. One would have to call it fate. Or even the Hand of A Merciful and Loving God. He's a wonderful man, Mr Fedallah.

ISHMAEL: But, sir—

BILDAD: That's enough, Mr…um.

ISHMAEL: Ishmael, sir.

BILDAD: I don't care. Just get back to work and see that you're not late again.

BILDAD exits. RACHEL enters. She carries a box, into which she begins emptying the items from her desk.

RACHEL: Hi, sailor.

ISHMAEL: Oh. Hi.

RACHEL: I missed you this morning. I woke up and you'd made a jump. What was so important that you had to pick up without saying au revoir?

ISHMAEL: Sorry. I…um…lost something important. and I

had to go to the hardware store and see if I could find the old man who sold it to me.

RACHEL: Did you find him?

ISHMAEL: No. That's the thing. The whole hardware store exploded just before I got there.

RACHEL: You're gaffing.

ISHMAEL: No, it was a big ball of hot flame. It was a mess.

RACHEL: Did you hear about Peleg? Isn't it Jonah's luck!

ISHMAEL: Yeah. Doesn't it seem fishy to you?

RACHEL: No. It did at first. But you should trunk up with Mr Fedallah! He's so charming! *(Beat.)* He wears too much cologne.

ISHMAEL: I beg your pardon?

RACHEL: Nanty. Good news. He bumped me up! He marched in this morning and flashed his ivories at me on his way to his office. Then that prick Bildad came out a few seconds later and said I was to be his personal assistant. And I got a raise! At the risk of barking my own turn, I'd say the new boss canvas man thinks I'm center ring!

ISHMAEL is at a loss. He eyes the mousetrap warily.

RACHEL: You're not green-eyed, are you?

ISHMAEL: Hm? Sorry.

RACHEL: That's okay. Why don't I come over tonight and we can celebrate?

ISHMAEL: Celebrate?

RACHEL: My promotion. Or last night, if you like. Maybe this time you'll stick around. We can have breakfast together. Unless you have an urgent chivaree at the stationery store or something.

ISHMAEL: I don't think that's a good idea. Not just now.

RACHEL: I don't get you.

ISHMAEL: Look, Rachel. I worship you. A lot. And the last thing I want to do is mess up what we have. But I'm a little worried about something at the moment, and I think maybe it's safest for both of us if you didn't come over for a while.

RACHEL: Safest?

ISHMAEL: There's something I need to sort out before we can be together.

RACHEL: You have a disease?

ISHMAEL: No. No! It's nothing like that. I just... It's really hard to explain.

RACHEL: If you're trying to break up with me, Professor, you're doing a really fink job.

ISHMAEL: I'm not. I...I don't know what to say.

RACHEL: Forget it. I'm Joey Grimaldi, I wouldn't understand. I have to go. Mr Fedallah needs to work, and our little parlare is holding him up. You know how to reach me when you've sorted it out. Until then, don't call me, Ishmael.

She exits. BILDAD enters.

BILDAD: Did she say your name was Ishmael?

ISHMAEL: Yes. She did, sir.

BILDAD: Pack up your things! You've been fired.

ISHMAEL: What?

BILDAD: You have fifteen minutes to vacate the premises,

then we're calling the police.[19] Mr Fedallah's orders!

ISHMAEL: Why? I've never even met this Fedallah. What have I done?

BILDAD: That's none of my concern. That's between you and him. But God help you if you've done something to hurt our sweet, saintly new boss! You'll have me to answer to! Now get out! Or getting fired will be the least of your worries! You vile heap of fly-caked rat-dung!

BILDAD exits. ISHMAEL gathers up his stuff.

Scene XVI

ISHMAEL knocks on his landlady's door.

ISHMAEL: Mrs Coffin! Mrs Coffin?

COFFIN: Go way. Mrs Coffin no home today.

ISHMAEL: I know you're home, Mrs Coffin.

COFFIN: No home.

ISHMAEL: I'm looking right at you. I can see you.

COFFIN: Coffin no home. Go way.

ISHMAEL: Mrs Coffin, the locks have been changed to my apartment. I can't open my door.

COFFIN: I evict you.

ISHMAEL: What?

COFFIN: You evicted now! Shooffa!

[19] This was what the president of the board of directors of the Stage Company in Penetanguishene said to the full assembled company when I was doing a production of *Nurse Jane Goes to Hawaii*. We had three sold out shows left to do. Strangest day I've ever had in a theatre. Seems the theatre had accounting issues.

ISHMAEL: You can't just evict me! You have to give me notice.

COFFIN: No notice. Evict you! You not living with under my roof!

ISHMAEL: Why! What did I do? My rent is paid. I'm a good tenant, you said so yourself.

COFFIN: Shekmiroska la semonelo! I know what you up to! What thing you do in you dark at night with under my roof! How do dare you say you do nothing! A nice man come by and warn me about you demented things you doing! We have word for you in my country! Bolshoyvakoska we call you! *(She spits.)*

ISHMAEL: I don't know what you're talking about? What man? Who warned you about me?

COFFIN: Mr Fedallah, He is warn me! He stop you. He stop all Bolshoyvakoska like you! He a good tenant, Mr Fedallah!

ISHMAEL: What do you mean, good tenant?

COFFIN: He move in today. He is much betterer in you room than you.

ISHMAEL: You gave my apartment to Mr Fedallah!

COFFIN: You go now or I call police!

He grabs her.

ISHMAEL: Wait, Mrs Coffin! You have to listen to me!

COFFIN: Help! Police! Bolshoyvakoska has me! Police come club him with you smukinovas! Help!

ISHMAEL releases her.

ISHMAEL: Mrs Coffin. Please. There's been a mistake. Something terrible is happening to me.

COFFIN: Mrs Coffin no home. Go way.

ISHMAEL: Fine then. I'll take it up with Fedallah.

COFFIN: He no home. He out to see a new lady friend. Shoofa!

ISHMAEL: What did you say?

COFFIN: I read his palm. They have destiny together.

COFFIN exits.

Scene XVII

RACHEL is on the phone.

RACHEL: Hi Mom! It's me!

MRS STUBB: Oh no. What's wrong? Are you in prison? Do you need me to post bail?

RACHEL: Nothing's wrong. I'm at home, safe.

MRS STUBB: Rachel, you can't fool your mother. If *you're* phoning *me,* some disaster has struck.

RACHEL: Mom, you're duking the bull's keister!

MRS STUBB: I'm what?

RACHEL: You're spieling the wrong plange! I have wonderful news! Come over, and I'll tell you all about it.

MRS STUBB: No Rachel, I don't think I could stand an evening of wild rumpus tumpus with you and your crazed bevy of roommates.

RACHEL: They aren't here. It's the strangest thing. There were these scratch and win tickets in with the mail this morning. Each of them won a trip to the Kokovokos! Except for Pippa, she swagged a trip to Japan. They flew out this afternoon. They left me a note.

MRS STUBB: Doesn't that sound fishy to you?

RACHEL: Mom, forget it. My news! Listen, I got a promotion this morning!

MRS STUBB: What are you now dear, Lady Manila Envelope, filing cabinet queen?

RACHEL: I am the personal assistant to the president of the entire company! And I got a raise! And the benefits, you won't believe! And a stock option! I don't even know what that is.

MRS STUBB: Rachel, really. I wasn't born in a cabbage patch.

RACHEL: Mom, it's strange and it's wonderful and it's true!

MRS STUBB: Oh. Oh. Oh my! Oh goodness, goodness, goodness! I am so proud of you!

RACHEL: You are? Mom, you never said you were proud of me before.

MRS STUBB: Of course I have. Don't be silly.

RACHEL: Well, I don't remember. I glad you're proud now. Please come over. I bought us some wine.

MRS STUBB: I'll be right over, sweetheart. You can tell me all about your new job.

RACHEL: And my new boss.

MRS STUBB: Is he handsome?

RACHEL: He is actually. But it doesn't matter. Mr Fedallah is my employer. Don't start doing flip-flaps.

MRS STUBB: My dreams are coming true for you, my sweet daughter.

An ominous knock.

RACHEL: My door, Mom. I gotta funnamble. *(Calling.)* Doors!

MRS STUBB: English , sweetie!

RACHEL: Right. *(Calling)* Come in!

MRS STUBB: I'll be right over. Darling. I love you.

She hangs up.

RACHEL: Wow. That's a fresh turn.

She opens the door. GRENDELMAUS stands there, disguised as a wealthy businessman. He wears stilts and a big, expensive suit, from which juts his tiny little mouse head. He speaks with a vaguely European accent.

Mr Fedallah!

GRENDELMAUS: Rachel, I had to see you.

RACHEL: Is something wrong at work, Mr Fedallah?

GRENDELMAUS: No, Rachel. This isn't about work. This is about you. I know we've only just met, but my soul is aflame. I fear to say this, lest you think I bandy the word about lightly, or without due consideration of its meaning, but I love you Rachel. I love you as I have never loved another. I feel like my heart has been locked alone and lonely in a dark and dusty chest, and the light of your eyes is the crowbar that has torn the hinges asunder and set it free. Now it beats naked and vulnerable, yearning for your nurturing arms to shield it from the wind and storm.

RACHEL: Mr Fedallah, I really wasn't expecting this. I thought you just wanted me to fax something.

GRENDELMAUS: Does love ever come from a place we expect? No. It comes unbidden from the shadowy corners, always a surprise.

RACHEL: My roommates will be home soon. Maybe we should talk about this tomorrow.

GRENDELMAUS: Your roommates won't be home till next Tuesday. They're in the Kokovokos. Except for Pippa, she's in Japan.

RACHEL: How do you know that?

GRENDELMAUS: I arranged the contest. I am a powerful man, Rachel. For me anything is possible. and I needed to speak to you, alone.

RACHEL: That's a lot of trouble to get me by myself. You could've hung out by the elevator till I left work.

GRENDELMAUS: It was a grand gesture to woo a grand woman. My influence is vast, Rachel. I wish to use it to make you happy.

RACHEL: This is crazy, you're my boss. I could have you on charges for work place harassment.

GRENDELMAUS: You could, and I might lose everything. But I would happily lose a kingdom, Rachel, for one brief moment in which I could lay my lips upon your soft cheek.

RACHEL: But you'd be banging your secretary. Isn't that a little, I don't know…improper?

GRENDELMAUS: Propriety be dammed! I want you, Rachel. I want you body and soul. I am a man of action, a beast. When I want something I seize it! That's enough now: No more talking!

He takes her in his arms and kisses her. She doesn't struggle.

RACHEL: But we hardly know each other.

GRENDELMAUS: I know you. I knew almost everything about you when I first gazed into your eyes. And what was still a mystery, I learned just now, when your fulsome lips opened to mine. You are just like me, Rachel, an old soul tired of wandering alone, searching for a companion, a companion who sets your body on fire, and who'll keep you warm on a winter's night.

RACHEL: I'm...involved with Ishmael.

GRENDELMAUS: You know in your heart that he can't give you what you need. He is too afraid of the world. I can make your every yearning a reality.

RACHEL: I don't want to hurt him. He has soft hands.

GRENDELMAUS: You want a beast. You know right now that you are mine.

RACHEL: This is wrong.

GRENDELMAUS: It is inevitable. Our love has been waiting centuries for this very moment. It's been ordained since Time first sprang forth from Eternity's womb.

RACHEL: Wow.

She kisses him. They embrace and move to the couch. He dims the light. From the darkness we hear...

RACHEL: Oh my God! What is that? Is that a tail?

GRENDELMAUS: Don't touch me there!

RACHEL: What is that? ...Oh God, what are you doing? Oh God yes. Mmm. Mmm-hm. Keep doing that.

Banging on the door.

ISHMAEL: Rachel? Are you in there?

MRS STUBB: Go away! She doesn't want to see you!

ISHMAEL: Rachel, it's me! I need to talk to you!

MRS STUBB: Leave her alone!

RACHEL: Just a minute. Oh Christ. I'm letting them in.

GRENDELMAUS: They can wait.

ISHMAEL: Rachel?

She turns on the light. Her clothes are askew. GRENDELMAUS's costume is amiss. ISHMAEL bursts in, followed by MRS STUBB. He sees FEDALLAH, and RACHEL and is dumbstruck.

MRS STUBB: I tried to stop him, honey! I was waiting outside your door. I wasn't listening. I just overheard you in here with you charming boss and I was waiting to hear how things went. And then he came up and demanded to see you.

ISHMAEL: Rachel?

RACHEL: Oh, no.

ISHMAEL: Who is this? How?

MRS STUBB: This is Mr Fedallah, you lazy masher!

RACHEL: Mother!

MRS STUBB: I'm going to phone the police.

RACHEL: No, don't do that.

ISHMAEL: Hey, don't I know you?

GRENDELMAUS: Perhaps. I have a haunting face.

ISHMAEL: No, I... *(He notices the evil stench!)* Oh God! It's you!

GRENDELMAUS: Da com of more under mist-hleothum
Grendel gongan Godes yrre baer!

MRS STUBB: What are they talking about dear?

ISHMAEL: Give me back my book!

RACHEL: Mother please stay out of this!

GRENDELMAUS: You're too late, you impotent fool.

ISHMAEL: Rachel, this can't be happening! Don't you know what he is?

RACHEL: Ishmael, please don't shout!

ISHMAEL: He's not even human!

MRS STUBB: He's crazy honey! I'll call the police.

ISHMAEL: Shut up!

RACHEL: Ishmael, please stay calm.

ISHMAEL: He stole...this...this thing from me, the night we...A book. And...I was supposed to use it on him. But you came over—! and wanted to...but—I couldn't because it... So...I used the book to help me! As an aid! Instead! and then he took it!

GRENDELMAUS: Rachel, he's obviously dangerous and deranged.

ISHMAEL: You dirty rat! You know I'm not deranged! *(To RACHEL.)* He had me evicted. And fired! He blew up the hardware store! And he's a mouse! Smell him! He stinks of mouse!

MRS STUBB: Some people will say anything!

GRENDELMAUS: Shall I remove him?

RACHEL: No!

ISHMAEL: I'll kill you with my bare hands! *(He lunges at GRENDELMAUS.)*

MRS STUBB: You savage!

ISHMAEL: I'll beat you to death with your your own arm!

Skirmish. RACHEL pries them apart.

RACHEL: Mr Fedallah. Stop please! You're killing him!

Skirmish ends.

GRENDELMAUS: You saw him. He's dangerous.

ISHMAEL: Rachel, you don't understand.

MRS STUBB: I told you this one was a good for nothing.

RACHEL: Mother, Mr Fedallah, will you leave us alone for a moment. I need to talk to Ishmael.

MRS STUBB: Darling, he just tried to murder Mr Fedallah!

ISHMAEL: He's a Mouse in a big suit! Is everyone blind but me!

RACHEL: I only need a minute.

GRENDELMAUS: We'll be waiting outside, if you need us, my Dear One.

They exit.

ISHMAEL: My dear one! He called you my dear one! This is unbearable!

RACHEL: I'm sorry, Ishmael. It just happened. Look, I know this is terrible. And I feel like pony flop for about what I'm going to say—

ISHMAEL: Then don't say it—

RACHEL: Mr Fedallah loves me. He wants me. He grabbed me in his arms and took me, and kissed me, and I felt alive, Ishmael. I feel like I've known him forever, like my body belongs to him. I'm his.

ISHMAEL: No.

RACHEL: And you saw how thrilled my mother is.

ISHMAEL: He's not what you think.

RACHEL: But this thing with you means so much to me. You've been my best friend for so long. Even those years I didn't see you. I don't understand it. Or you. I don't know what it means. But I don't want to give it up.

ISHMAEL: Then don't.

RACHEL: That's not enough. What do I mean to you, Ishmael? I need to know.

ISHMAEL: A lot. Everything. I don't know. In high school, I used to imagine us growing old together. We'd be smiling. And sitting on a park bench, holding our baby.

RACHEL: And now?

ISHMAEL: I can't...look...Carl Jung has this theory about the anima, and the animus and the shadow. And I think this whole situation here—

RACHEL: I don't care what you think. I need to know what you feel. What do I mean to you now?

ISHMAEL: He's a Mouse!

RACHEL: Make me stay with you.

ISHMAEL: He's a Mouse.

Silence.

RACHEL: Ishmael, I'm sorry. This isn't going to happen.

ISHMAEL: This can't be real.

RACHEL: I need to be with Mr Fedallah now. Maybe I'm making the biggest mistake of my life, and someday, I'll wake up from a dream and your name will be on my lips. And then I'll come find you. But I don't think so, Ishmael. I think this is the end for us.

ISHMAEL: I'm not giving up.

RACHEL: You already did.

She holds her ground. Silence. He exits.

Scene XIX

ISHMAEL is alone, forlorn and destitute. OLD MAN enters and puts his hand on ISHMAEL's shoulder.

OLD MAN: I've been searching for ye, m'lad.

ISHMAEL: You're too late. Everything is too late.

OLD MAN: The Grendelmaus ist a fearsome foe.

ISHMAEL: I looked for you at the hardware store, but it exploded.

OLD MAN: Ay. A small white paw struck the flint, which set that fuse alight.

ISHMAEL: I lost your book. He took it. I'm sorry. Then he took my job. And my home. And now he's taken the woman I love.

OLD MAN: Ye art accursed, Boy. The dry land ist no place for ye now. While ye tread upon the same soil as the Grendelmaus, he shall rule over ye and blow ye down. All the Earth is his.

ISHMAEL: What do I do?

OLD MAN: Art ye man enough to slay the fiend with yer bare hands.

ISHMAEL: I don't think so.

OLD MAN: Then ye must run and hide till ye art man enough.

ISHMAEL: Where can I go?

OLD MAN: Follow my lead, Lad. Do as I did when the fell beast purloined my young limb and sign aboard a schooner. Take solace in the briny bosom of the salty deep.

ISHMAEL: I promised someone I would do that once.

OLD MAN: Then go ye to sea. Let that cold, watery strumpet keep ye until Mother Earth seest fit to welcome ye with loving arms again. Till that far off day, the world is not for ye. Ye Peckerhead.

Black out.

Epilogue

RACHEL sits by the puppet theatre. It's empty.

RACHEL: Twelve years passed. Rachel and the Mouse were married. And it was wonderful. The sex was amazing, and life was a rollercoaster. A high wire without a net. She thought she'd be happy for a long time. She was falling no more, fate had caught her in its net. But as the years went on, she grew less sure. The things about her husband that were once daring and erotic started to feel dangerous and unearthly. Sometimes when they fought, which was a lot, his yellow eyes would flash violently. And she'd notice his pointed teeth. And remember Ishmael's warning, and the sad look on his face, and then she would wonder where he was, her sweet friend Ishmael. Twelve years is a long time to wonder about someone you've lost.

She is sitting on a bench by the water, rocking a small baby wrapped in swaddling clothes. ISHMAEL enters. He is older, and dressed in the garb of a merchant marine. He carries a duffle bag over his shoulder and looks weary.

RACHEL: Ishmael? Is that you?

ISHMAEL: Rachel Stubb?

RACHEL: Rachel Fedallah. Yes. It's me.

ISHMAEL: Isn't that funny. My first day back, and I see you.

RACHEL: Where have you been? Sometimes I thought I saw

you. But it was never you.

ISHMAEL: I signed aboard ship as a deep sea fisherman. I haven't stood on solid ground since…since I last saw you. I wanted to find adventure on the high seas. But it's like you said, it sounds exciting when it's someone else's life, but when it's yours, it's just life. Last week I woke up, looked at the water and thought, "Time to be a lubber again. Time quit the sea and come home."

RACHEL: I hurt you that badly, did I?

ISHMAEL: No. I just needed to go somewhere and grow up a little. I don't remember it very well any more.

RACHEL: I do. I remember it very well.

ISHMAEL: Are you and that…Fedallah still together?

RACHEL: Yes. I left him once. But I went back. It's hard to let go, you know.

ISHMAEL: Yeah. I do. I'm sorry.

RACHEL: It's okay. Marriage is supposed to be hard, right?

ISHMAEL: At least you're working through your problems together.

RACHEL: We're not really. We just keep them all buried under the floorboards, and act like strangers…like ghosts who haunt each other's house. Every once in a while, we take our problems out and fight about them for old time's sake. To remind ourselves that we're connected. How's that for healthy?

ISHMAEL: I don't know. I've been chasing fish around the ocean for twelve years. I'm not really one to judge. If some brave Ulysses crawled out of the ocean to take you away from it all, do you think you'd go?

RACHEL: Depends on the Ulysses. He was the smart one right? I've had it up to here with Hectors and Agamemnons.

ISHMAEL: Is that your baby?

RACHEL: Yes. This is Starbuck. He's six. He hasn't grown much yet. The doctors don't know why.

ISHMAEL: He's cute.

RACHEL: Really? I think so. Fedallah's funny about him. I don't think he's very paternal. Once I came into the nursey and I swear Fedallah was trying to eat him.

ISHMAEL: May I hold him?

RACHEL: Sure.

As ISHMAEL takes the baby, the swaddling falls away to reveal the baby is a grotesque mouse-human hybrid. ISHMAEL sits beside RACHEL.

ISHMAEL: Hello little sailor.

RACHEL: He likes you.

ISHMAEL: I still think about you.

RACHEL: I still think about you too.

RACHEL and ISHMAEL touch hands. GRENDELMAUS's shadow appears behind them. Slow fade to black.

The End.